THE CALL TO RADICAL DISCIPLESHIP

Are You Really A Christian?

"A Christian is not about doing religious things; it is about being a righteous person."

By Dr. Charles L. Wilson

Published by
CrossHouse Publishing,
P.O. Box 461592
Garland, Texas 75046-1592
Printed in the United States of America
by Lightning Source, LaVergne, TN

ISBN 978-1-934749-21-0

~Acknowledgements~

I know that God has brought special people into my life to help me be conformed to Christ's image. I can't speak of being a disciple of the Lord Jesus without thanking some of these people that have made such contributions to me.

To Muril and Jewel Wilson, my blessed parents who have been such mentors in my life. They truly have instructed me in the paths of God.

To L.A. Murr, one of God's statesmen who has inspired me as a model of one who loves the Lord and seeks to place Jesus first in all he does.

To my wife, Paulette and my brother, Milburn Wilson who have partnered with me, assisting me in making a difference in the lives of hurting people.

To Michael Bridges, my spiritual partner in ministry, and Juan Reyna who has been a trusted friend and supporter. Lastly, to Cliff Jenkins who has been the iron that has helped sharpen my life.

How blessed I am to have served alongside so many dear people through these years of ministry. A complete list of these saints would contain many pages.

~Dedication~

To Beverly Gibbons, who has contributed so much to my life, and her husband Bill who is a constant source of support. None of my literary efforts would have been possible without her.

To Bruce Ray Kassab, my fellow pastor who is so gifted by God. He has given insightful commentary and editing to my manuscripts.

To Brad Harrison, who does so many things as Executive Pastor to allow me to have the time to attempt writing the things God has placed upon my heart.

To Roger Dimsdle, who has been my prayer partner over these past 20 years. He has made a great contribution to my life.

Table Of Contents

Introduction

When Jesus came to preach the Sermon on the Mount, He was becoming famous. He was preaching like no one ever had preached; "As one having authority." He performed miracles, the crowds were growing into what I like to call, "Christ followers." But that is all they were. They were uncommitted to the call of being a disciple of Jesus Christ. They were there for the excitement, the entertainment, and the enticements. Jesus was not looking for a crowd, but was looking for those who would understand the kingdom message and commit to Him as His disciples.

To change their world the disciples had to be radical in their commitment. The crowd had the wrong idea about what God was up to. It was not about miracles, but ministry. It was about taking up their cross and following Jesus. It was about personally giving their lives in exchange for His life; to live for eternity, not the present.

Jesus' message was, and always will be, counter-cultural. It says that the call to discipleship is a call to change our value system, to break from the bondage of this world's system. The only way to do that is to no longer want what the world offers. Only then can we be truly free in Christ and live a life of fulfillment of which we have never dreamed.

I want to reflect back upon an incident that happened in our youth ministry in which a student had been a continual problem and disruption. I was called upon to correct the behavior. I confronted the young man and he openly became very belligerent. I said to him, "If you don't straighten up you will have to leave." He defiantly said, "Who cares!" I responded, "If you have to leave you will not be allowed to attend future youth functions." He responded, "Who cares!" I continued, "If you can't come to other activities, that also means you can't attend youth camp!" Once again he reiterated, "Who cares." I had nothing he wanted so I had no power over him.

In a positive way that's exactly where we as believers have to get to in order to be a faithful and fruitful disciple of the Lord Jesus. We have to look at the world's stuff and say, "Who cares." When we can say that we are ready for the call to be a radical disciple.

If I have something you want, I have control over you. A professor offering the promise of a pocket full of good grades can influence a student to read books they don't want to read, go to classes they don't want to attend, and take tests for which they don't want to prepare. When the student no longer wants the grade, however, the professor's influence and power is gone. No wonder Paul warns us not to be conformed to this world. But we will be conformed until we no longer want the world. We must reject its false promises and unfilled claims. Only when we believe and act upon the truth are we free from the power of this world.

The problem is the culture has created artificial wants. I say "artificial' because nothing in the world can bring true happiness and inward joy. Unfortunately, the culture's artificially created wants have become more important to the average person than their real personal needs. That's why the prophet said, "We spend our money on that which does not satisfy." This has always been the way of those separated from God.

To be really free is to be free from the domination of culture, meaning we no longer want what the system says we have to have, but instead we want the Kingdom of Christ.

Only when our lives are centered upon Christ and we love God more than our current world system that brings disappointment, despair and destruction, can we become radical disciples of Christ.

The Sermon on the Mount calls for believers to step across the line and to live a different lifestyle. It's more than believing in God; it's believing God. This book is a cry for radical change in the church. It's a plea to stop performing and start professing our only hope. That hope is to be totally committed to loving God, following His example, and seeking to model His life.

Before we can deal with the characteristics of a true disciple of Jesus as set forth in the Beatitudes and Sermon on the Mount, I feel we must define a disciple. Jesus beautifully gives us a description of what a disciple looks like in the Gospel of Luke, chapter 14, verses 25-35. The definition of a disciple is someone who learns from his master. The word "disciple" means learner. When we learn from our teacher, then we will be like our teacher. Jesus' commands to the world can be summed up in two phrases, "come unto me," and "come after me."

Growing up in church we often sang, "It pays to serve Jesus; it pays every day." May I also say it costs to serve Jesus. It costs every day, and it costs every step of the way. I hope that the mention of cost doesn't scare you off. It costs, but it is well worth it.

When a person commits to being a disciple of Jesus Christ they need to come with their eyes wide open. We, as His disciples, are not called to share in Jesus' popularity, but His unpopularity. The writer of Hebrews says, ***"Let us go forth, therefore, unto Him without the camp, bearing His reproach." (Hebrews 13:13)*** To be a disciple of Jesus Christ may not bring you medals; it may even bring you scars.

When Garibaldi set out to liberate Italy he saw a group of young men on a street corner and asked them to follow him. "What do you offer" they asked. "Offer? I offer you hardship, hunger, rags, thirst, sleepless nights, foot sores, and long marches, innumerable privations, and victory in the noblest cause that has ever been asked of you." They followed him to total and complete victory.

Jesus paints clear pictures of what His disciples must be. For instance, Jesus points out that a disciple is one who worships God at any cost. ***"If anyone comes to Me and does not hate his father and mother, wife and children, brothers and sisters, yes, and his own life also, he cannot be My disciple. And whoever does not bear his cross and come after Me cannot be My disciple." (Luke 14:26-27)***

I mentioned that there is a cost. It is a cost of personal relationships. Jesus certainly is not calling upon anyone to hate his parents and family. To love Jesus causes us to truly love others more. The word "hate" is used here by Jesus meaning to "make a clear choice." Later on in the sermon (Matthew 6:24), Jesus points out the impossibility of serving God and having anything rival God in our lives. Jesus must come before all human relationships. He demands and deserves unrivaled love. ***"He who loves father or mother more than Me is not worthy of Me. And he who loves son or daughter more than Me is not worthy of Me. And he who does not take his cross and follow after Me is not worthy of Me." (Matthew 10:37-38)***

There is a cost of personal reputation. Notice the words "his own life." This is not talking about self-denial, but denial of self. There is a difference in these two statements. A person can deny themselves things without denying themselves. Peter forsook his nets long before he forsook himself.

Churches today have become self-service cafeterias. Self-esteem seems to be their main goal. The focus has moved toward how to be self-fulfilled and simultaneously the flesh is promised pleasure, pride, and glory. May I say just because a generation wants to let culture set the tone for worship does not mean it is what God wants. Every generation has wanted that. In the past men of God have stood for truth and not caved in to tolerance. In fact, the popular Christian term "seekers" is by definition a population that doesn't really even know what they are seeking until the truth is proclaimed! In this passage Jesus is going to talk about taking up a cross. A cross was a sign of shame and reproach in Jesus' culture. The Bible says Jesus made Himself of no reputation. How unlike that is to so many in the church who want to be Christian superstars.

There is the cost of personal renunciation; that is to "bear His cross." When a person comes to Jesus as a disciple they have made their last independent decision. I read of a young man coming to A.W. Tozer, the great man of God who taught the deeper life, the crucified life, and asking, "What does it mean to be crucified in Christ?" He responded, "Well, to be crucified means three things:

- The man who is on the cross faces only one way
- The man who is crucified is not going back.
- The man on the cross has no future plans and agendas.

A second picture of Jesus' description is that a disciple must work at any cost. ***"For which of you, intending to build a tower, does not sit down first and count the cost, whether he has enough to finish it— lest, after he has laid the foundation, and is not able to finish, all who see it begin to mock him, saying, 'This man began to build and was not able to finish'?" (Luke 14:28-30)*** Discipleship is a life of kingdom building. There is the crucifixion to the old world that is followed by a construction of a new life. The tower in the middle of a vineyard speaks of protection and fruitfulness. The disciple's life is a life of spiritual conviction. Rather than asking

God to bless what he is doing, the disciple prays and asks God that he might do what He is blessing. Disciples of Jesus seek God to be the architect of their lives. God has a plan for our lives, yet too many are drawing their breath, drawing their salary, gulping down a meal, rushing to a job, fighting traffic, coming home, turning on a television program, and calling it a day without ever consulting God's Word or praying to God for direction.

The life of a disciple is spiritually conceived and it is also sacrificially constructed. Jesus said "count the cost." There is no cheap way or lazy way to spiritual growth. The disciple steadfastly seeks to grow in Christ. Paul said, ***"I have fought a good fight; I have finished my course, I have kept the faith." (2 Timothy 4:7)*** Paul was faithful to the fight, faithful to the faith, and faithful to the finish.

There is nothing but heartbreak to half-built towers. The Bible has a lot to say about quitters and nothing about them is good, or pleasing to God. A lot of Christians who are continuously shopping for a church are actually demonstrating their lack of commitment to the cause of Christ.

A third portrait Jesus gives of His disciples is that they <u>war at any cost</u>. ***"Or what king, going to make war against another king, does not sit down first and consider whether he is able with ten thousand to meet him who comes against him with twenty thousand? Or else, while the other is still a great way off, he sends a delegation and asks conditions of peace." (Luke 14:31-32)*** To be a disciple not only means a crucifixion and a construction, it also means a conflict. A disciple understands they are in spiritual warfare for a while. Let me say Jesus wants warriors who are not cowards. The odds look overwhelming. Many Christians are like the little boy who said, "I would like to be a soldier and go off to war and fight battles if I knew I wouldn't get hurt." Rather, we should be like the military officer surrounded by the enemy who announced to his troops, "Don't let any of them escape."

Jesus' warriors are not cowards and they are not compromisers. We don't need to be ambassadors that strike up an agreement with the devil. We cannot peacefully coexist with Satan. If we do not win in this spiritual war, we lose it all. John MacArthur said, *"In war there is no substitute for victory."* I think the motto of the French Foreign Legion applies, *"If I falter, push me on; if I stumble, pick me up; if I retreat, shoot me!"*

Finally Jesus helps us picture the disciple as one who witnesses at any cost. ***"Salt is good; but if the salt has lost its flavor, how shall it be seasoned? It is neither fit for the land nor for the dunghill, but men throw it out. He who has ears to hear, let him hear!" (Luke 14:34-35)*** The disciple of Jesus understands that they are commissioned. We are called to be salt and light. Salt speaks of our witness and testimony. Too many so-called disciples have a testimony that is flat. There is no zest and flavor to it. A true disciple will be like salt.

In Jesus' culture salt was very valuable. As a matter of fact the Roman government would sometimes pay its soldiers in salt. That's where we get the saying, "Someone is worth or not worth their weight in salt." Why was it so valuable?

Salt is a preservative that prevented decay and restrained corruption of food. Our culture is in need of the preserving power of a salty gospel. How sad it is in our culture that sodomy has gone from a sin to a sickness, to a socially accepted practice. The cesspools of iniquity are full and running over; love has been forsaken for lust, Satan is worshipped as a god, and man has magnified himself above his maker. The only problems in our world are not Hollywood, pornographers, liquor dealers, drug pushers, politicians or the theological liberals. A major problem is saltless Christians who call themselves disciples.

Salt is valuable because it flavors; it causes flavor to come alive. One little boy said, "Salt is what tastes bad when you don't have it." God has called us to flavor our world, yet most people in the world live flavorless lives. They are not all that interested in going to heaven or hell; they simply want to know how to hack it on Monday. Yet too many of us offer them a tasteless faith and a flat testimony; it becomes a case if the "bland leading the bland."

Salt also has healing properties to it. Elisha threw salt into a poisonous spring and healed the water. True disciples turn barrenness and bitterness into blessedness. The salty gospel can heal broken homes, broken hearts and broken hopes. Of course, salt burns before it heals. God's truth, when rubbed into this diseased culture, will sting and burn. The curse of letting the world set the atmosphere for the church is that they want the non-irritating brand of religion. They had rather have money than salt. Listen, no offense means no effect. We need to stop trying to win a popularity contest. Not everyone will appreciate salty saints.

The powerful truth is this; salt penetrates. Put a pinch of salt in a jug of water and all the water becomes salty. It's not enough to sit in our salt shakers on Sunday. We have become the power to influence our world for God, but it has to be spread into the culture.

Salt in biblical times came from the Dead Sea. The sun evaporated the water and left behind the salt and minerals. If left to itself and exposed to humidity, the bite of the salt leached out and left the chemicals and impurities. It becomes valueless and even harmful. You couldn't throw it in the field because it would kill the plant life. If it drained into the well, it would contaminate the water. The only other thing to do was to throw it on the hard rocky pathway and let men walk on it. ***"You are the salt of the earth; but if the salt loses its flavor, how shall it be seasoned? It is then good for nothing but to be thrown out and trampled underfoot by men." (Matthew 5:13)***

When we as professors of Christ lose our saltiness, we ought not be amazed when we are trodden under foot by a godless world. Much of the Christian bashing we see today is because of saltless saints. It's my prayer that this book will not only give us a new challenge as Christ's disciples, but we will gain insight as to how to present the salty gospel and live salty lives for Christ!

~Poor In Spirit~

"Blessed are the poor in spirit, for theirs is the kingdom of heaven." (Matthew 5:3)

If I were to say that you are a backslider, it is unlikely that it would bother you too much. I could even call you a sinner and I doubt you would be offended. But if I were to say to you, "You're a fool" most people would be deeply offended. Yet Jesus said if a person does not hear and heed His words he is a fool. To know that there is a storm coming and not prepare for it would be foolish just as building your home without a foundation would be foolish. I see our world full of fallen people living in a fallen culture. That is, of course, because we have become foolish. The Bible says, "The fool has said in his heart there is no God." Yet Jesus carries that statement even further. He said to hear and not listen to His words makes you a fool because it carries with it its own consequences. Most people would never say, "There is no God!" Yet most people, many even in the church, live as if there is no God. They pay little or no attention to what God has said in His word.

I know the argument, "I don't believe the Bible is God's Word." Listen, you don't have to believe the Bible for the Bible to have authority upon your life. It is alive and powerful. If you will listen it will authenticate itself. It will transform your mind and bring you to Jesus.

The Sermon on the Mount defines to us what it means to be a disciple of Jesus Christ. The Beatitudes define the fully committed disciple, and the sermon describes the lifestyle of the disciple.

A tragedy of our day has been the gross misinterpretation of what it means to be a disciple of Jesus Christ. This false presumption is in direct contrast to the teaching Jesus gives in this sermon.

The church over the last sixty years has so watered down the gospel and carnalized Christianity that most people don't understand what it means to come to Jesus. What impresses most of us does not impress Jesus.

The Beatitudes tell us what Jesus is impressed with, with each of these principles growing out of the other. There is an order to it, a foundation to our salvation and consequently our being a disciple of Jesus Christ. By the way, every child of God is a disciple. It's not optional.

Jesus begins by saying the disciple of Jesus is <u>poor in spirit</u>. Nobody in Jesus' day or in our day is interested in being poor. As a matter of fact, the reason they were following Jesus was for what it brought to their lives physically and materially.

What does it mean to be poor in Spirit? Well, it does not mean simply being poor. There is nothing about poverty that is godly. Poor people are not holy because of their poverty.

When God created man He created him in entirety: body, soul, and spirit. God made his body and in that body He placed a spirit. Then He breathed life into Him and he became a living soul.

With the body we have world consciousness. We can live in and relate to this physical world. With our spirit we have self-consciousness; a self-awareness of who we are, that we are alive. It is our soul, made up of our emotion, will, and intellect that allows us to connect to God. It gives us a God consciousness. It is our soul that enables us to communicate with God and to know God. The soul is who we really are. It's what sets mankind apart from the animal world. Animals have bodies and spirits, but they have no soul, therefore, they have no consciousness of God. They can't know God. When God sees man He is not looking at our bodies, but our souls; the real us.

To be poor in spirit means that our self-consciousness knows there is no way that our dead soul can have life by our own effort. Just as animals are separated from God and are helpless to change their condition, people, without God live like an animal and cannot change their condition anymore than a leopard can change its spots. But with "God consciousness" people stand before God and know that they are absolutely poor.

Jesus' message devastates worldly attitudes. We cannot fill our empty dead soul with eternal things. Nothing can bring life to the soul but God. Jesus came to announce that the tree of happiness does not grow on the cursed earth. Physical things do not touch the soul of man. We cannot fill a spiritual need with a physical substance.

Being poor in spirit is man's attitude of himself in the presence of a holy God. No one struts before the Lord. We are like Lazarus in Luke 16; we are a beggar before God with nothing to offer.

Many come to God with the attitude, "I know I'm not perfect, but I am not all that bad. I am as good as most people." We are like the rich young ruler who felt he only lacked one thing; his life was so good he was almost perfect, but he was as close as it gets. They believe they are a sinner but that is not all they are. Jesus is saying you are a sinner and that's all you are.

Paul said in Romans 7:18, ***"In my flesh dwells no good thing."*** He was a beggar before God. What does that mean?

First of all, a beggar is conscious of his need. I don't think there is a beggar in the world who doesn't know they are a beggar. Jesus said it all begins by having the right attitude about sin. Being poor in spirit is the very first thing that must happen in the life of anyone who ever enters God's kingdom. Nobody ever entered on the basis of pride. The doorway is very low, and only people who crawl can come in.

Sadly, in cultural Christianity there is little of the self-emptying concept. There are many books on how to be successful but not on how to be a nobody. Poverty of spirit is the foundation of all graces, yet so much of modern Christianity feeds on pride. This is obvious in how Christian celebrities are so highly promoted. Listen, you might as well expect fruit to grow without trees if you think the graces of the Christian life grow without humility. As long as we are not poor in spirit, we cannot receive grace. You can't become a Christian unless you are poor in spirit. As you live your Christian life, you will never know the other graces as long as you refuse to experience poverty of spirit.

Jesus says it starts here; happy are the humble. Until we are humble, Christ is never precious to us. We can't see Him when we are looking only at ourselves. Because we see our own desires, needs, and desperations, we never see the matchless worth of Christ. Until we know how damned we are, we cannot appreciate how glorious He is. Until we see our poverty, we cannot understand His riches. In our deadness we come alive. No man ever comes to Jesus Christ and enters the kingdom without crawling, without a terrible sense of sinfulness and repentance.

God gives grace to the humble. That's why a poor spirit has to be at the very beginning. The only way to come to God is to confess unrighteousness, confess inability to meet God's standard, and confess that you cannot do it. You enter with a sense of helplessness and desperation to receive divine blessing, and maintain that sense in order to know continual happiness as you live in Christ.

How many fools there are in the world who never see the truth. Even Christians who come to God with the right attitude have been swept into the modern world's exaltation of the individual. The emerging church puts man in God's place and downplays the very Word of God. The words of a young preacher still rings in my ears, *"Don't you know preaching is more about performance than teaching?"* Be a star, draw a crowd, and start your own show because it's all about you! No, it's not! It's all about Jesus!

God identifies with people who beg on the inside, not people who are self-sufficient; not people who think they can work out their own salvation. Poor in spirit does not mean poor-spirited in the sense of lacking passion and enthusiasm. It does not mean being lazy, quiet, indifferent, or passive. An individual who is poor in spirit is one with no self-sufficiency. We see the classic illustration in Luke 18:9-14, ***"He also told this parable to some who trusted in themselves that they were righteous and looked down on everyone else: Two men went up to the temple complex to pray, one a Pharisee and the other a tax collector. The Pharisee took his stand and was praying like this: God, I thank You that I'm not like other people —greedy, unrighteous, adulterers, or even like this tax collector. I fast twice a week; I give a tenth of everything I get. But the tax collector, standing far off, would not even raise his eyes to heaven but kept striking his chest and saying, God, turn Your wrath from me —a sinner! I tell you, this one went down to his house justified rather than the other; because everyone who exalts himself will be humbled, but the one who humbles himself will be exalted." (Luke 18:9-14)***

James wrote, ***"Humble yourselves in the presence of the Lord, and He will exalt you." (James 4:10)*** This is not a poverty against which the will rebels, but rather it is a poverty under which the will bows in a deep dependence and submission. This is not popular doctrine in the Christian culture today. We emphasize celebrities, experts, superstars and the rich and famous Christians. But happiness is for the humble.

Religions are man's answer to the call to be poor in spirit. There are three things that God hates about our religions.

• First of all, religion does not go <u>deep enough.</u>

"For I tell you, unless your righteousness surpasses that of the scribes and Pharisees, you will never enter the kingdom of heaven. You have heard that it was said to our ancestors, Do not murder, and whoever murders will be subject to judgment. But I tell you, everyone who is angry with his brother will be subject to judgment. And whoever says to his brother, 'Fool!' will be subject to the Sanhedrin. But whoever says, 'You moron!' will be subject to hellfire." (Matthew 5:20-22)

Most people have the religion of the Pharisees and it looks great. But it is a surface appearance. We evaluate ourselves on the basis of external actions. We see ourselves as good because of some things we have done. Jesus is saying your standing before God is not based on external actions. The Lord searches the heart.

"For the word of God is living and effective and sharper than any two-edged sword, penetrating as far as to divide soul, spirit, joints, and marrow; it is a judge of the ideas and thoughts of the heart. No creature is hidden from Him, but all things are naked and exposed to the eyes of Him to whom we must give an account." (Hebrews 4:12-13)

Religions look on the outside, but God knows your heart. God is not only looking at our <u>deeds</u>, but our <u>desires</u>. Listen, if we were judged by the court system of our land based on our desires, we would all be convicted no matter what image we portray.

• Secondly, religion does not go <u>far enough</u>.

"And if anyone forces you to go one mile, go with him two. Give to the one who asks you, and don't turn away from the one who wants to borrow from you." (Matthew 5:41-42)

The law said you had to go one mile. Jesus said disciples are willing to do more than you have to do. Most Christians are careful not to do more than they have to do to get by. I see it in pastoral staffs, deacons, Sunday School teachers, as well as lay people in general. Did you know that only five percent of church attenders tithe? Ten percent of the people serve in ninety percent of the ministries in the average church. That's not the disciple Jesus was talking about.

• Thirdly, religion does not go high enough.

We find so many times that religion compares. It's not comparing yourself to someone else. Do you know why a person has to be born again? Why are we condemned by God? Because God judges us against His standard of being perfect; His own nature. If you are not as good as God, you are lost. The Bible says that without holiness no man will see the Lord. When I realize this I see I am a beggar; totally dependent upon God for life. God will not bestow blessings upon your life until you acknowledge who He is and who you are.

When I was a child we used to have beggars come by our house and ask for food. I still remember them having very little. Our family comparably looked very wealthy. They walked down the road having received food from my mom. If that man would have come to our door in a suit and parked by the road in a car, he would not have gotten food from my mom. That would have been a joke to us. Religion helps people put on an image of something they are not. Religion is not an honest portrayal of the person's condition.

When we remove the veil of self-righteous religion, God can use us. Jacob had to face the poverty of spirit before God could use him. He fought God all night, and finally God dislocated Jacob's hip. (Refer to Genesis 32). He put him flat on his back. Then the Bible says in Genesis 32:29, ***"And He [God] blessed him there."***

Isaiah could not be used before he was poor in spirit. He lamented the death of King Uzziah and was thinking of only his loss when God graciously invaded his life and showed him what really mattered. He showed Himself high and lifted up in a vision and Isaiah said, ***"Woe is me, for I am ruined! Because I am a man of unclean lips…for my eyes have seen the King." (Isaiah 6:5)***

Gideon became aware of his inadequacy. He said, ***"Oh my Lord, wherewith shall I save Israel? Behold my family is poor in Manasseh, and I am the least in my father's house." (Judges 6:15)*** But God said you are a man of valor. Do you know who the mightiest man of valor is? The man who knows that in himself he is impotent.

That was Moses' heart. He was so desperately, horribly and fearfully conscious of his inadequacy and his insufficiency, that God used him to lead His chosen people. It was the heart of David who said, ***"Who am I, O God, and what is my house, that you have brought me this far?" (2 Samuel 7:18)***

We see it with Peter, who was aggressive, self-assertive, and confident by nature. Yet he said, ***"Go away from me Lord, for I am a sinful man, O Lord!" (Luke 5:8)*** The Apostle Paul recognized that in his flesh dwelt no good thing. He was the chief of sinners, a blasphemer, a persecutor. He admitted in humility everything he had was garbage compared to who God was. All things he counted loss. He was sufficient for nothing.

The world says, *"Assert yourself, be proud of yourself, grab your place in the sun."* But God says that when you admit your weakness, when you admit your nothingness, that's not the end. It's the beginning! But it's the hardest thing you will ever do.

So how do you know if you are poor in spirit? I was once told that when you can say you are humble, you're not. The question is hard to answer, however, consider the following:

• When you are poor in spirit life is no longer about you. You are focusing on Christ and His glory and about others and their needs.

• The person that is poor in spirit thinks about God's plan and purpose and desires the smile of God upon their life more than anything else.

• The person poor in spirit knows a contentment that is not concerned with what they do not have, but is grateful for what they do have.

• The person poor in spirit wants Christ more than anything. He is so desperate that he will give up anything just to have Christ, the hidden treasure and pearl of great price.

• The person poor in spirit is one who is overwhelmed that God's grace has been given to him.

A few years ago I was diagnosed with cancer. The thing I discovered is that a person can be very ill and not even know it. I had a potentially life-threatening disease but did not realize I was sick. The same thing is true spiritually speaking. The majority of our population is walking around with the life-threatening disease of sin and do not realize the severity of their condition. Without Christ they are spiritually dead. Cancer can kill your body but sin can kill your soul. That disease of sin affects every area of your life and those who are tied relationally to you.

What Is Unhealthy In Your Life?

Pace of life	Diet	Finances
Thought-life	Worries	Relationship with . . ..
Work life	Habits	Anger
Marriage	Family	____________
Addictions	Memories	____________
Expectations	Regrets	____________

These are all symptoms of the real problem of being separated from life in Christ by sin. Have you accepted the fact that sin has made you who you have become? This first Beatitude says, "You are not God!" I must admit I'm powerless and helpless to control my tendency to do what I know is unhealthy and admit my life is unmanageable. Paul describes us all in a sense, ***"I don't understand myself at all, for I really want to do what is right, but I can't! I do what I don't want to, what I hate! I know perfectly well what I'm doing is wrong…but I can't help myself." (Romans 7:15; 17, LB)***

- Do you ever stay up late when you know you need sleep?
- Do you ever eat things that you know you shouldn't?
- Do you ever make commitments that you can't possibly keep?
- Do you ever feel you should exercise but you don't?
- Do you ever try to control something you know you can't?

The Bible calls the tendency to do what we know is unhealthy, "our sinful nature." We all have one. This means we have a natural inclination to do things that we know are self-destructive, even though we know they are bad for our lives. The wisest man in the world, Solomon said, ***"There is a way that <u>seems right</u> to man but its ways ends in death." (Proverbs 16:25)***

Jesus begins the Beatitudes by saying our greatest problem is "playing God" in our life. We not only want to control our lives, but to control the people and circumstances around us. We think we know more about what is best than anyone, including the Word of God. Listen, when God says, "don't," He is saying, "Don't hurt yourself." Yet everyday we make choices and decisions that say, "I am smarter than God! I know what God says but I'm going to do something different instead! I know what the Bible says but I believe going this direction is better for me."

We believe we know more about life than God who created and gave us life and we willfully disobey Him. The prophet warns, ***"In the pride of your heart you say, I'm a god…but you are just a man and not a god, though you think you are as wise as a god." (Ezekiel 28:29)***

The heart of being poor in spirit is recognizing there is a God and I am not Him. We play God in very unassuming ways:

• By denying our humility (problems, pains, faults, and failures).

• By trying to control everything.

The more insecure we are the more we do these two things. The more we deny that we have a problem, the more we cover up and try to hide our insecurities by attempting to control everyone and everything. The more out of control we are the more desperately we try to control people and situations around us. How?

• By denying our problems: "I can handle this; I know what I am doing; I can quit anytime."

• By controlling other people: Out of using guilt, shame, anger, threats, or promises.

• By avoiding our pain: By self-medicating ourselves, shopping, overeating, or illicit affairs. We all have our own "medicine" that we use.

We don't like who or what we are, so we try to remake ourselves, but it only makes our problems worse. The Bible asks, ***"does not the potter have power over the clay, from the same lump to make one vessel for honor and another for dishonor?" (Romans 9:21)***

The consequences of playing God are:

• Frustration***: "It seems to be a fact that when I want to do what is right, I inevitably do what is wrong, but there is something else deep within me, my lower nature, that is <u>at</u>***

***work with my** mind and wins the fight..." (Romans 7:21; 23)* There is such frustration to fail in life by messing up and there is such frustration in not being able to do any differently than we have done. The more we pretend we are in control, the more frustrated we will become.

• Fatigue: The Psalmist said, ***"My strength evaporated like water on a sunny day until I finally admitted all my sins to you and stopped trying to hide them." (Psalm 32:4-5)*** Denial will suck the life out of you. We can never hide from the fact that we are sinners; just ask Adam. Our lives are naked and open before God. We know that God knows!

• Failure: Listen to God's Word, ***"You will never succeed in life if you try to hide your sins. Confess them and give them up; then God will show mercy to you." (Proverbs 28:13)*** Because we don't want to fail we wear masks, play games, and try to cover up. After all, in our culture, image is everything.

How Do I Become Poor In Spirit?

The first step is we must admit we need God's help. This means:

• We admit we are powerless to changing our past; no matter how much we regret or resent it.

• We admit we are powerless to controlling other people. We can only be responsible for ourselves.

• We admit we are powerless to changing our unhealthy habits on our own.

"We saw how powerless we were to help ourselves; but that was good, for then we put everything into the hands of God, who alone could save us for He can even raise the dead." (2 Corinthians 1:9)

The second step is to humble ourselves before God as the

Lord of our life. This means I totally surrender my will to God's will. Did you know that humility of heart increases our happiness? It reduces our stress. We no longer have to have all the answers. We are now depending upon God, even when things are not ideal.

Secondly, it improves our relationships. Nobody wants to be around a conceited jerk. They are a pain in the blessed assurance. Self-centered people are never happy people. On the other hand when a person becomes interested in others, they become interesting to others.

Finally, it releases God's power in our lives. The Bible declares, ***"God gives grace (power under God's control) to the humble, but sets Himself against the proud." (James 4:6) "When we were unable to help ourselves, at the moment of our need, Christ died for us!" (Romans 5:6)***

The prophet proclaims, ***"God gives power to the faint, and strengthens the powerless." (Isaiah 40:29)***

That's why Jesus begins here. I love the *Philip's Translation* of this Beatitude, ***"Happy are those who know their need for God, for the kingdom of heaven is theirs." (Matthew 5:3)***

I must humble myself before God, not because I need God to let me go to heaven when I die; I need Him because I have to live on earth today. If you are saying, 'I pass on God; I can make it on my own," then I say, "Good luck!" He will also let you face eternity alone. But if you want God and God's power, He will supernaturally give it to you through a personal relationship with Jesus Christ.

Jesus said, ***"Now that you know the truth, how happy you will be if you put it into practice!" (John 15:17)***

~Godly Sorrow~

"Blessed are those who mourn, for they shall be comforted." (Matthew 5:4)

The Beatitudes are the seed; the Sermon on the Mount is the flower. Jesus lays out the attitude of every one of His disciples. In the Beatitudes Jesus is defining what it is to be a Christian; in the Sermon on the Mount He shows how the lifestyle is demonstrated. The true disciple of Christ is broken over their sin. That's not a picture of most people who fill the church pews each week.

When man wants to build a better life, he seeks to change the conditions and circumstances because he believes conditions will make better lives. That's the culture's philosophy. When God seeks to make a better life He changes the person's character. The major difference in the thinking of man and the mind of God is this. Man believes that changed conditions will improve character. God knows, however, that only changed character will improve conditions. Man works on the outside, the external, the image, and seeks to gain entrance to the inside. God starts on the inside and when the man is right on the inside he will be right on the outside. That is the real difference between religion and real salvation. Religion focuses on the outside; it is ritual, rules, and conformity. That's why this sermon is so essential.

God's primary focus has never been on conditions. When Jesus was here in His earthly ministry, He was not into social reform as we know it. Man will compromise convictions and disobey God's laws in order to improve his own circumstances and conditions.

When Jesus was on earth in His ministry there was a great moral evil present, and yet Jesus did not say one thing against it. That moral evil was slavery. Why didn't Jesus address such an evil? Because that was a symptom and not the problem. We spend all our efforts on the symptoms. Was slavery wrong? Of course. Jesus knew that the issue was an issue of man's heart, not the eternal sin of enslaving his fellow man. If the heart is unchanged, man will just gravitate to a worse evil.

You can move people from the ghetto to the penthouse and in a matter of time that penthouse will start to resemble the ghetto. Why? Because you can't change the character of a man by changing his conditions or circumstances.

There is more than one way to kill a tree. You can chop it down or completely remove its bark, but either way the tree is going to die; it's just a matter of when. What Jesus did was strip the bark from slavery and it killed it as certain as anything.

If Jesus would have only abolished this evil condition, and He could have, in all likelihood even worse conditions would have replaced it. In our country we desire to abolish racial discrimination and prejudice. We have merely sought to change the conditions. Let me ask you, "Do we still have racial hatred today?" We have changed the conditions so that it is hidden, but it still lives on today. There remains racial inequality; it's just masked. Why? Because character has not changed. This is why we must expose the real issue. The issue is the lack of transformed lives. The Christian is different, therefore, he changes culture. For example, when you find true disciples of Christ you will find a school, a hospital, an orphanage, or a homeless shelter, and there you will find equal rights. But it is the changed character that changes the conditions, not the other way around.

So Jesus describes for us who is a real disciple and who is only a follower of Christ. It begins with being spiritually bankrupt before God. He has nothing that enables him to come to God. He is hopelessly separated from God and is dead in his sin.

The second reality grows out of the first. We mourn over that reality. Our sin has separated us from God, His will, His purpose, and His plan for our life.

In Psalm 55, one of the songs of David shows how broken he is over the pain his heart knows in the disappointment and the sorrows of life. ***"Oh that I had wings like a dove! I would fly away and be at rest. Behold, I would wander far away, I would lodge in the wilderness, I would hasten to my place of refuge from the stormy wind and tempest." (vs. 6-8)***

We all know what it is to have sorrow, and I am sure none of us like that feeling. Yet Jesus said mourning brings happiness. Why? Because God Himself will comfort us. The wrong sorrow only brings pain and little comfort. We seldom mourn for the right things. Sometimes we mourn because we can satisfy our lust. At other times we are like Amnon, who is 2 Samuel 13 wept because he could not satisfy his lust to defile his own sister. We weep and mourn over a bad economy. In the Book of Revelation when God literally is judging the world because of their sin, the world is weeping, not because of their sin, but because business is off. We weep over our team losing the championship. I am sure you see what I am talking about. We try to cover it and keep it inside, but we mourn when our will is violated and we don't get what we want.

The Bible says in 2 Corinthians 7:10, ***"For the sorrow that is according to the will of God produces repentance without regret, leading to salvation, but the sorrow of the world pro-***

duces death." You can cry your eyes out about your problems, and you can weep all you want about loneliness, about discouragement, about disappointment, out of earnest love. You can also cry about your unfulfilled lust. When it is all said and done, none of that worldly sorrow will bring you life. It will not bring you comfort.

Only one kind of sorrow brings life, and that is godly sorrow, which leads to repentance. Therefore, we can conclude that Jesus is referring in this Beatitude to sorrow over sin. Godly sorrow is linked to repentance, and repentance is linked to sin. This kind of mourning means being sorry because you are a sinner. You can't hide that sorrow. The disciple's life is characterized by mourning over sin.

Jesus is saying that when you are bankrupt before God you are broken in your heart. What a different perspective from most of us who attend church today. We want to be entertained. We want to be made to laugh and feel good. What contrast I see in where we are and where God wants us to be.

The Prophet Jeremiah said that Israel had lost its ability to blush at sin. They had lost their sin consciousness. Listen, if we can laugh at sin we will soon accept it. Let me ask you, "Do you accept sin today that you would have run from in the past?" We are a culture of tolerance. That tolerance has found its way into the church. Our church is filled with tares, and we are losing our sin consciousness. Therefore, God is not able to do His work in our lives. James said, ***"Let your joy be turned to heaviness and your laughter turned to mourning." (James 4:9)*** We need to weep when we see our spiritual bankruptcy. That's where revival has always started.

We don't hear about repentance today, but there is no conversion without it. Why should we be broken over our sin? Because of the penetrating power of sin. ***"You have heard that it was said, 'Do not commit adultery.' But I tell you, everyone***

who looks at a woman to lust for her has already committed adultery with her in his heart." (Matthew 5:27-28) Jesus said immorality is not just in the act, but in the desire. What condemning words are these, ***"...already in his heart!"*** Here is a man who has a desire for impure things. He thinks because he has never physically acted upon it he's alright. We think sin lays upon the surface of our lives like lint on a dark blue suit and it can just be picked off. It's not like that. Sin is like lye soap that eats into the tissue of our heart. Many would say they are a disciple because their surface life is good in appearance. Jesus said out of the heart are the issues of life. The heart is desperately wicked.

By his own testimony concerning the law Paul was above reproach. But in Romans 7 we see that while outwardly he conformed to rules, his desire was wrong. I doubt if many priests have ever heard in confession, "I am covetous." Why? Because we are not convicted over our sinful desires if we don't act upon them. We evaluate our lives solely on surface Christianity. Sin penetrates our very being. We try to compensate by telling people we are Christians. We do the "acceptable" things, such as going to church, giving an offering, reading the Bible, or praying when trouble comes. This is why rules and religions will not help. ***"Such rules are mere human teachings, for food was made to be eaten and used up. These rules may seem good, for rules of this kind require strong devotion and are humiliating and hard on the body, but they have no effect when it comes to conquering a person's evil thoughts and desires. They only make him proud." (Colossians 2:22-23)*** This is rulebook religion. It has no power to transform the evil desires of the heart. It only makes them proud. The Pharisees were conceited and proud in their self-righteousness. They were not broken over their sin and, therefore, condemned by Jesus.

In Psalm 32 David wrote, ***"when I keep silent about my sin, my body wasted away through my groaning all day long. For day and night your hand was heavy upon me…"*** Compare that to the words of Nehemiah who walked with God, ***"And the good hand of God was upon me." (Nehemiah 2:18)*** David found relief and said, ***"I acknowledged my sin to you, and my iniquity I did not hide; I said, I will confess my transgressions to the Lord; and you forgave the guilt of my sin." (Psalm 32:5)***

Regarding the same sin, David said, ***"Be gracious to me, God, according to Your faithful love; according to Your abundant compassion, blot out my rebellion. Wash away my guilt, and cleanse me from my sin. For I am conscious of my rebellion, and my sin is always before me. God, create a clean heart for me and renew a steadfast spirit within me. Do not banish me from Your presence or take Your Holy Spirit from me. Restore the joy of Your salvation to me, and give me a willing spirit." (Psalm 51:1-3; 10-12)***

Secondly, we should mourn over our sin because of the perverting power of sin. ***"If your right eye causes you to sin, gouge it out and throw it away. For it is better that you lose one of the parts of your body than for your whole body to be thrown into hell.*** 30 ***And if your right hand causes you to sin, cut it off and throw it away. For it is better that you lose one of the parts of your body than for your whole body to go into hell!" (Matthew 5:29-30)*** Jesus saw that the characteristic of sin is that it takes that which is good and perverts it so badly that you would be better to pluck out your right eye or cut off your right hand than to have it. Why the right eye and the right hand? Because in biblical terms the right hand has the emphasis, therefore, the most important. The eye is an example of the pleasurable things; the hand represents the useful things of life. In some countries if you steal they cut off your right hand.

God is saying here that the right eye and the right hand are the most precious gifts from God. But sin takes your most precious gifts and perverts them into your own destruction. God gives good gifts. The greatest evils today in our culture are the good gifts of God that have been perverted: sex, drugs, our families, our potential, and our youth. Sin twists and perverts the good things of God into evil and it destroys instead of blesses.

If you don't take your sin seriously, it will take the most precious things you have and twist them. The dysfunctional home is now the norm. Households are no longer places of security and rest, because a family member's sin has turned them into nightmares. Sin perverts. The Bible says, "The way of transgression is hard." If you have a lifestyle of sin you are not a disciple, regardless of whether you attend church or not.

We ought to mourn over our sin because of the perishing power of our sin. Sin kills! It brings forth death. Sin ultimately brings men to hell and eternal separation from God. It will damn your soul to hell.

Mourners are happy because they are the only ones who are forgiven. The rest of the world has to live with endless guilt. Notice the Bible doesn't say God will console the mourner. He doesn't say, "Now, now, it will all be alright!" No! He comforts those who are broken and repentant over their sin. ***"Draw near to God, and He will draw near to you. Cleanse your hands, sinners, and purify your hearts, double-minded people! Be miserable and mourn and weep. Your laughter must change to mourning and your joy to sorrow. Humble yourselves before the Lord, and He will exalt you." (James 4:8-10)*** So many Christians spend all their lives trying to find happiness. They get counseling, read a book, or attend a support group, when what they really need to do is mourn over their own sin. God will comfort them and Jesus said they will be happy; not in the sense of "ha ha" happy but in the sense of a deep and abiding peace, having a right relationship with God.

The comfort God gives us brings us hope. Hope is the light at the end of the tunnel. It is the expectation that God is at work in your life and that gives you the necessary energy to stay with it.

Jesus is saying when we are broken over our sin God will bring us comfort that makes us happy. How does God comfort those who mourn over their sin? First of all, He reminds us of His presence in our lives. Job said in Job 8:11, ***"Those who forget God have no hope."*** Listen, if there were no God we should be discouraged. Most people intellectually know God exists. There is little comfort in just believing in God. Most people are practical atheists, not intellectual atheists. A practical atheist is one who believes God exists, but lives as if He did not. They don't consult God's Word, they don't pray, and they certainly don't endeavor to make God first place in their lives. Therefore, they are not true disciples. I love the words of Psalm 94:19, ***"Lord, when doubts fill my mind, when my heart is in turmoil, quiet me and give me renewed hope and cheer."*** Are you living with a consciousness of God's presence?

Secondly, God's comfort is letting us know He cares; God loves us and we matter. I have hopes when I think of this, ***"The Lord's love <u>never ends</u>; His mercies never stop; they are new every morning." (Lamentations 3:21-23)*** Human love can die because man's love is conditional, but God's love is unconditional. God says, ***"I have loved you with an everlasting love." (Jeremiah 31:3)***

Let me ask you; in your sorrow over sin have you let God love you? You know about God's love, but have you experienced His unconditional love? Most of us think God only loves us on our good days, but that He frowns upon us on our bad days. The Psalmist says of God, ***"He is like a father to us, tender and sympathetic…for He knows what we are made of – dust." (Psalm 103:13-14)*** My favorite title for God is "Heavenly Father." That means He is not just a father in image, but He is a perfect father. Everything in heaven is perfect so Jesus says, "God is a perfect heavenly Father." Listen, if God loved you as a sinner, how much more can we rejoice in His love as a son!

As a Heavenly Father we find comfort in that He knows our situation. When I was growing up at the news hour the statement was made on television, "It's ten o'clock, do you know where your children are?" The answer was in many cases, "no." But God knows where you are, how you got there, and He loves you completely. The Bible says, ***"You know how troubled I am; you have kept a record of my tears." (Psalm 56:6)*** That is unbelievably personal. He has not missed anything about you with His eternal eye of compassion.

God not only knows, but He cares. David prayed in Psalm 31:7, ***"…you have seen the crisis of my soul."*** When I am broken over my sin I don't have to fear God because He is not working against me, but for me.

We have hope in God because He not only cares, but He has power to bring into our life that which we do not have. The Bible repeatedly reminds us, ***"What is impossible for man is possible for God." (Luke 18:27)*** Because God's power is unlimited, nothing can keep Him from working in our lives. Paul said of Abraham, ***"When everything was hopeless, Abraham believed anyway, deciding to live <u>not</u> on the basis of what <u>he could not do</u>, but on what <u>God said He would do</u>." (Romans 4:18)*** Most things in life are beyond our control, therefore, we are <u>helpless</u>, but we are not <u>hopeless</u>; because God has power that we do not have! Paul said, ***"For***

God is at work within you, giving you the will and the power to achieve His purpose." (Philippians 2:13) We have a "higher power" and His name is Jesus Christ. He is not just a power; He is a person and He wants to have a personal relationship with us.

Ron Dunn used to say, *"Leaves do not fall off dead trees."* This is so true. Do you know why leaves fall off trees? They fall off because there is life in the tree. When the new life moves up the trunk of the tree into the branches, the old leaf is pushed off for the coming new leaf. When I am mourning over sin, there is comfort in knowing that because of the Christ-life the sins that break my heart are being replaced with the righteousness of God through Christ.

What comfort there is in knowing God is present in my life and He has promised to help me. David said to God, ***"I expect your help, for you have promised it." (Psalm 119:81)*** The Bible says in Hebrews 6:18, ***"God cannot lie when He makes a promise, and He cannot lie when he makes an oath. These things encourage us…they give us strength to <u>hold on to the hope</u> we have been given."***

The result of God's presence, provision, and promise is that the sad will be comforted. John said, ***"My little children, these things I write to you, that you may not sin. And if anyone sins, we have an advocate with the Father, Jesus Christ, the righteous." (1 John 2:1)*** The word advocate is just as easily translated "comforter." When we are broken over our sin, there is one who will stand beside us who will be our advocate. He will intercede on our behalf, He will strengthen us and He will meet our need.

In the Book of Galatians, Chapters 5-6, Paul deals with the war that rages in every one of us; the flesh vs. the spirit. Paul calls them the <u>works</u> of the flesh, and the <u>fruit</u> of the spirit. Works are what man does, but fruit is the natural process and product of the Christ life. In Romans 15:15, Paul says this, ***"May the God of hope fill you will all joy…that by the power of the Holy Spirit, your life and outlook may be radiant with hope."*** I love that. That's comfort. The Bible says in 2 Timothy 1:7, ***"The spirit that God gives us…fills us with power, love, and sound mind or self-control."***

We need power. If we could have changed we would have. We need love; the ability to establish deep, meaningful, lasting relationships and we need to be able to think clearly and have the discipline of self-control. This is not simply my ability to control myself; it is rather self-under God's control. This brings the ability to say, "No" to self-destruction, and "Yes," to God's plan and purpose for our lives. The comfort of being a disciple who mourns over their sin is:

- The comfort of a Father's pardon.
- The comfort of a Savior's peace.
- The comfort of the Spirit's power.

~Power Under Control~

"Blessed are the meek, for they shall inherit the earth." (Matthew 5:5)

One of the characteristics of a real disciple of Christ is meekness. The Bible, in Numbers 12:3, says that Moses was a man of meekness. He was not a man of weakness, but meekness. ***"Patience is better than power, and controlling one's temper, than capturing a city." (Proverbs 16:32)*** Solomon, the wisest man who ever lived, had insight into what it meant to be meek. A meek man is a man with the ability to control his spirit. He said it is easier for a man to take a city than it is to control his own spirit.

A phrase that defines our culture is, "out of control." That cannot define the life of a disciple. Jesus said the Christian disciple is like a stallion that has been broken. A domesticated horse has not lost his power or spirit. The only difference between the wild stallion and the domesticated saddle horse is that the domesticated horse is controlled by a master. All his power, energy, and abilities have been channeled for a purpose.

Texas and Oklahoma are major horse states. Horses are a part of their very culture. They know the value of a trained horse. Can you imagine the value of a cutting horse whose response is immediate and perfectly in tune to his master who sits in the saddle? From the pressure of the rider's knee the horse responds in split-second obedience. That horse is what my grandfather used to call a "meeked" horse. The animal has spirit, power, and speed, but all that is under the control of his master.

God wants to domesticate every disciple. What does that mean? A meek person is gentle, mild, tenderhearted, patient, and submissive. The word meek was often used in scripture to describe a soothing medicine, a gentle breeze, a colt that had been broken and domesticated. It was used to describe the characteristic of Jesus in 2 Corinthians 10:1 and Matthew 21:5. ***"Behold, thy king cometh unto thee, meek, and sitting upon an ass, on a colt the foal of an ass."*** When Jesus came into the city, He was riding, not on a white stallion, but on a donkey. He was meek, but not weak. Power under control is the by-product of self-emptying, of self-humiliation, of brokenness before God. It is the taming of the lion.

Meekness does not mean impotence. ***"Like a city that is broken into and without walls is a man who has no control over his spirit." (Proverbs 25:28)*** In other words, a person has power but no control over it. It's like a destroyed city. To rule the spirit is meekness.

The man of meekness is not running around trying to get his due. He's already broken in spirit over his sin, and he's already mourning and weeping over the consequence of it. In humility he stands before a holy God and he has nothing to commend himself.

This is not cowardice or wishy-washy lack of conviction. It's not just human niceness. Meekness says, "In myself, nothing is possible, but in God, everything is possible." It is not a passive acceptance but a holy indignation over the things of God and thereby places that righteous anger under control. Peter said, ***"For you have been called for this purpose, since Christ also suffered for you, leaving you an example for you to follow in His steps, who committed no sin, nor was any deceit found in his mouth." (1 Peter 2:21-22)*** Christ never did anything wrong, so whatever anyone accused him of was false. His life was above reproach.

Jesus never defended himself, but when people desecrated His Father's house of prayer he made a whip and beat them. He hated only what the Father hated and loved only what the Father loved. Meekness says, "I have no defense for myself, but I will die defending God!"

Jesus blasted the hypocrites and confronted and condemned false religious leaders. He fearlessly spoke truth to the crowds. Meekness is power under control.

• A meek person is God controlled.

"You have heard that it was said, An eye for an eye and a tooth for a tooth. But I tell you, don't resist an evildoer. On the contrary, if anyone slaps you on your right cheek, turn the other to him also…You have heard that it was said, Love your neighbor and hate your enemy. But I tell you, love your enemies and pray for those who persecute you…" (Matthew 5:38-39; 43-44)

This is counter-cultural. It cuts against the grain of human nature. Jesus contrasted human nature and God's will. Most of us evaluate our Christianity by how we act. God evaluates our Christianity by how we react to negative circumstances. It's not how you act, but how you react that shows whether or not you are a real disciple of Jesus. It is easy to <u>act</u> right; it is very difficult to <u>react</u> right. That requires a life under the control of the Holy Spirit.

Have you noticed in a sports competition it is easier to act right when you are ahead on the scoreboard? It's easier to be gracious when you are ahead. When I am behind, it's harder not to be upset. Meekness says we are to allow Christ's life to so dominate our mind that we react as Jesus did.

To be meek is to live a life of denying self. Notice I did not say self-denial. Listen, I can practice self-denial and not be filled with God's Holy Spirit. It is dying to self. ***"…and I no longer live, but Christ lives in me. The life I now live in the flesh, I live by faith in the Son of God, who loved me and gave Himself for me." (Galatians 2:20)*** Meekness means I am not sensitive about myself. The most miserable person in the world is the person who is super-sensitive about himself. They evaluate everything in terms of themselves. Life always has to be about them. The person full of themselves is not a very big person. A meek person is someone who is not self-absorbed, but God-absorbed; one who is not so concerned for themselves but totally concerned about God.

• A meek person is love controlled.

"But I tell you, love your enemies and pray for those who persecute you, so that you may be sons of your Father in heaven. For He causes His sun to rise on the evil and the good, and sends rain on the righteous and the unrighteous." (Matthew 5:44-45)

Can you imagine what people felt when Jesus said the disciple of Jesus is one who loves their enemy? Jesus is not referring to an emotional feeling, but a God kind of love. A God kind of love for people is treating your enemy as if he were your friend. Jesus said God treats people the same. God lets everyone have sunshine and rain. He responds in kindness and not retaliation. To bless a person model Christ before them.

• A meek person is eternity controlled.

The person who is not self-controlled will fight and struggle to get every thing coming to him in this life. How foolish because the Bible says that the world is in the process of passing away. Listen, the world is falling apart, and cutting gas emissions will not change that. The Bible says the world is passing away but he that does the will of God abides forever. The result of having your focus on heaven will first of all bring happiness. There will be an abiding, true joy, based on an eternal relationship with the living God.

A second great result of being eternity controlled is that the meek shall inherit the earth. We will inherit paradise regained. We will rule and reign with Christ. The word inherit means to receive an allotted portion. God promised it and laid it out. Psalm 37 included a very definite promise of the Lord, and yet the righteous among the Jews were saying, "Well, why do all the evil people prosper while we are getting the dirty end of everything?" The Psalmist responded in effect, ***"Don't you worry about that, you just commit your way to the Lord, trust only in Him, delight in Him, and He will give you the desire of your heart." (Psalm 37:4)*** Psalm 37:13 says the Lord, ***"…laughs at him, for he sees his day is coming."*** It may look like it has reversed now, but he says those people, those evil doers shall be cut down like grass, and they shall wither like the green herb. ***"For evildoers will be cut off, but those who wait for the Lord, they will inherit the land." (Psalm 37:9)***

The true disciple will be there as part of that kingdom. ***"So no one should boast in men, for all things are yours: whether Paul or Apollos or Cephas or the world or life or death or things present or things to come —all are yours, and you belong to Christ, and Christ to God." (1 Corinthians 3:21-23) "For the Lord takes pleasure in His people; He adorns the humble with salvation." (Psalm 149:4)***

One day God will execute vengeance on the nations. He will bind their kings with chains and their nobles with fetters. The world as we know it now, the world as we see it now is in escrow. We will be established in the millennium to rule and reign with Christ. And while we are alive right now, the Bible lists many benefits of meekness.

- ***"The meek shall be satisfied." (Psalm 22:26)***
- ***"The meek He will guide and teach." (Psalm 25:9)***
- ***"The meek become wise." (Proverbs 11:2)***
- ***"The meek will be filled with joy." (Isaiah 29:19)***

Why is it that we shy away from meekness? As a kid my generation read comic books. The back cover was used for advertisement. Often they advertised bodybuilding products and would have a picture of a Charles Atlas looking guy on a beach kicking dirt on a 90 lb. weakling, stealing his girlfriend. The meaning of this ad was, "If you take this product, in three months you can be a bully too!" I seriously doubt they would have received too many orders if the ad would have approached it like this, "Are you tired of pushing people around? Are you tired of picking on 90 lb. weaklings or being a bully? Send for this equipment and you can become a new person and know the joy of meekness!" No one wants to be weak, so no one wants to be meek.

The disciple of Jesus Christ is meek. They understand that meekness is letting go and letting God. It is surrendering and submitting to what God wants to do in our lives. God has given us passions, abilities, ambitions, and desires. They are real and they motivate us. But we are like a car in this sense. A car can drive down the road to its destination or it can run into a brick wall to its destruction. It will in either case get the same gas mileage, perform the same. The manufacturing company designs the car with a steering wheel so that someone who knows the difference between destination and destruction can guide it. Unless we submit to God's rule and control, we are going to run our lives into destruction and despair because we don't have the right perspective any more than a monkey can drive a car.

The Marks Of Meekness

First of all, meekness means we make Jesus the manager of our lives. I don't know any professing Christian who does not want Jesus in their life, but I do know few who really want

Jesus to be Lord in their lives. I read a sign once that said, *"I would rather change my mind and succeed than have my own way and fail."* A meek person is one who has had a change of will. The Bible says, ***"Stop quarreling with God! If you agree with Him, you will have peace at last, and things will go well for you." (Job 21:21)*** That's the secret of the successful disciple. That is meekness. The disciple no longer usurps God's authority over their life. The value in the disciple's life is allowing God's plan and purpose to be fulfilled in their life. Jesus said to those potential disciples, ***"Anyone who intends to come with me has to <u>let me lead</u>; you're not in the drivers seat; I am…"*** That is Matthew 16:24 out of The Message Bible. Dr. Peterson is right on in his translation. Most Christians are what I would call, "Back Seat Christians." They want to tell God what direction He can go in their lives. To most professing Christians, Jesus is only a figurative headship in their lives. He is like the king or queen of England. They are the formal head of leadership, but it is the parliament who has all the power and authority. We declare Jesus to be Lord and sovereign authority, but we run the government of our lives.

The authority of Jesus in our lives must become a once and for all decision. I often tell youth that the time to make your decision concerning moral purity is before you go on the date, not when you are alone in a parked car with passions heated and glands out of control.

When I was in the Army I served during the Vietnam War. While training we were shown actual footage of battle in hand-to-hand combat. We had taken great losses in this area. The drill instructor told us it was because we who were raised in the United States were taught a high value on human life. The Vietcong placed little value on human life. When we found ourselves in hand-to-hand combat we made individual choices about whether or not we would take another's life as we looked into their face. In that split second we were deciding we were not going to die because the enemy had already made a lethal decision. A real disciple makes up their mind once and for all, "I am going to submit and surrender to God's plan and purpose for my life. No matter where my life leads or what circumstances I face, the decision has been made like Joshua in the Old Testament." ***"As for me and my house we will serve the Lord." (Joshua 24:15)***

Secondly, meekness means we establish God's Word as the authority for our lives. James commands us to, ***"Place yourself under God's authority." (James 4:7)*** Everyone will struggle with realizing proper authority over their life. There will be many voices yelling at us, opinions offered, and agendas presented to us. However, only God's Word is a knowledgeable authority. Warning signs in life are placed there by authorities because they see the big picture. For example, traffic signs on highway entrances and exit ramps might read, "Do not enter." Those signs are not placed there to ruin your life, but to keep you and others safe and traffic flowing. To disregard that sign is to put your life and others' lives in peril.

When God's Word gives instruction it's for our blessing and the world's benefit. When God says, "Don't," He is saying, "Don't hurt yourself and others." God's words are instruction and rules for living life. If you ignore them, you will be hurt.

By what authority are you living your life?

- Popular opinion?
- Your mate?
- Your children?
- Your desires, appetites, or drive?
- Your addictions or habits?
- Your ego?

Everyone is controlled by something. God's Word is to control the disciple of Jesus Christ. Listen to what Paul told Timothy concerning God's Word. ***"All scripture is inspired by God and is useful to teach us what is true and to make us realize what is wrong in our lives. It straightens us out and teaches us to do what is right." (2 Timothy 3:16)***

- The Bible teaches us what is true.
- The Bible makes us realize what's wrong in our lives.
- The Bible straightens us out.
- The Bible teaches us to do what is right.

God's Word does not change. Jesus never changes and man's deepest needs never change. During an interview before Allen Shepherd, an astronaut in the United States Space Program was going to be shot into space and a reporter asked, "On what are you depending upon most?" He replied, "That God's laws will not change." Truth never changes. God's divine laws never change, so we can build our lives upon the Bible's authority. David said, ***"I <u>have made up my mind</u> to obey your laws forever, no matter what." (Psalm 119:112)*** He continued, ***"I will never lay aside your laws, for you have used them to restore my joy and health."*** Have you made that once and for all decision?

Another characteristic of meekness is that the disciple embraces God's Spirit as the power of their life. The prophet Ezekiel said in Ezekiel 36:27, ***"I will put my spirit in you and enable you to live by my laws."*** The Holy Spirit energized the disciple of Jesus with power under God's control. The message in the Bible reads like this in Galatians 3:10, ***"anyone who tries to live by his own effort, independent of God, is doomed to failure."*** Paul goes on to ask, ***"…if you begin your life in Christ by the Spirit. Now are you trying to make it complete by your own power? That's foolish!" (Galatians 3:3)*** God gives His disciples both the will and the power to live life.

Paul said, ***"I have the strength to face all conditions by the power that Christ gives me." (Philippians 4:13)***

Finally, the meek disciple is marked by the characteristic of keeping Jesus as the focus of their life. The writer of Hebrews says, ***"We must keep our eye on Jesus, who leads us and makes our faith complete." (Hebrews 12:2)*** Spiritually speaking, many believers suffer from spiritual A.D.D. We are so easily distracted. We start down the road of obedience and recovery, but then we relapse back to our old hurts, habits, and hang-ups. We stop looking at Jesus and begin focusing on lesser things.

Our lives always move toward that upon which we focus. When I was in Drivers Education one student asked the instructor, "How do you stay in your lane?" The instructor said, "Focus your gaze 100 yards ahead, look at the center of your lane, and you will automatically go there." That's also true in life. We go to where our focus is. That's why David said, ***"If I keep my eyes on God, I won't trip over my own feet." (Psalm 25:15)*** Solomon said, ***"Listen for God's voice in everything you do, everywhere you go; He's the one who will keep you on track." (Proverbs 3:6)***

For centuries sailors navigated by setting their course by the North Star. The disciple of Christ has Jesus as their North Star because, like the North Star, He does not change. Meekness means my focus is stayed upon Jesus. He is my guiding light. Solomon also said, ***"The payoff for meekness…is plenty and honor, and a satisfying life." (Proverbs 22:4)*** The reality of this message is that we all surrender control of our lives to something or someone. Perhaps it's a person, a habit, a hurt, a hang-up, an ambition or drive. Let me ask you, has what you surrendered control of your life to up to this point brought you what you really want? Or has it betrayed you and left you empty and regretful?

A disciple of Jesus is a person who has discovered that meekness pays off because Jesus will never disappoint. Only God can totally fulfill your life.

~Hungry For God~

"Blessed are those who hunger and thirst for righteousness, for they shall be filled." (Matthew 5:6)

Our culture is in a famine; and starving people will eat anything. It is not a lack of physical food, but a lack of spiritual truth. It is as the prophet foretold; a famine for the truth of God's Word. This has always been the circumstance for fallen men, but it is very pronounced today. The Bible is filled with examples of people who were hungry for the wrong things. There was Lucifer, Nebuchadnezzar, the rich fool, and the list goes on and on. There is nothing wrong with ambition, passion, a resolute drive, or great desire, if it focuses on the right thing.

What is the right thing? A hunger for God's righteousness. Food and water are necessities and here Christ is saying you need righteousness like you need food and water. Our physical lives depend upon food and water; our spiritual lives depend on righteousness.

Today in parts of Africa, India, and Latin America, thousands die each day from malnutrition and the diseases it brings. But all the hunger in the world grows pale in comparison to the unfulfilled spiritual hunger and unquenched spiritual thirst.

Unsaved people thirst for happiness and hunger for fulfillment, but as it has been said, they seek for it in all the wrong places. In fact, Peter compared the unsaved to a dog that licks up its own vomit or a pig that wallows in its own mire. (See 2 Peter 2:22). The heart of every person in the world was created with a hunger for God. Solomon said, ***"God has set eternity in our hearts." (Ecclesiastes 3:11)*** But man tries to satisfy hunger for God with things that can never satisfy. The prophet Isaiah said in Isaiah 55:2, ***"He seeks that which is not bread."*** Jesus said, ***"I am the bread of life…" (John 6:35)*** He told the woman at the well in John 4 that He was the water that would satisfy her thirsty soul. The prophet Jeremiah identified the crisis of man's hearts, ***"they have forsaken Me, the fountain of living water, to hew for themselves cisterns, broken cisterns that cannot hold water." (Jeremiah 2:13)***

The Apostle John warns that satisfaction is in nothing the world offers. ***"don't love the world nor the things in the world…the lust of the flesh, the lust of the eye, the pride of life…" (1 John 2:15-16)*** None of these last. It's just wind. Those who respond to the spirit of God come running back to the Father and there is a feast to fill the empty heart.

Moses' Discovery

The true disciple of Christ settles the life question that disciples have always had to settle. In Hebrews Chapter Eleven we have the list of those faithful followers of God. In that list Moses stands out, as perhaps the greatest man of God in the Old Testament. Why? Because he was settled on who his faith was in. There are four questions that true disciples have to settle:

- Who am I?
- What are my choices?
- What is really important?
- What are my goals?

The first is an identity crisis. Moses was born a Hebrew

but raised in the Egyptian Palace. If he said I am an Egyptian, he would have a life of fame, fortune, and influence, but if he said I am a Jew, he would become a slave and be ruled over. ***"By faith Moses, when he had grown up, refused to be called the son of Pharaoh's daughter." (Hebrews 11:24)*** He refused to live a lie. He chose to be what God had designed him to be. When you say yes to God you automatically say no to many other things. There is a cost to being a disciple. Listen, while God chose Moses as a child, when he grew up he had to choose God. That's our question today. God has chosen you but are you willing to choose God? Notice Moses chose God when he grew up. One of the marks of maturity in life is that you accept responsibility for your life. Our culture loves to blame everyone and everything for the direction of our lives. You can't live off other people's commitments. Moses had to make a choice by accepting personal responsibility. Nobody can ultimately ruin your life but you, not even Satan. His power is limited to certain ends. God will not ruin your life because He loves you. The only one who can ultimately mess up your life is you. The mature believer says I choose God's will and plan for my life over my will and my agenda.

The second question is about establishing a value system for your life. ***"Considering the reproach of Christ greater riches than the treasure of Egypt, for he was looking to the reward." (Heb. 11:26)*** Moses considered God's will as of greater value than all the treasures of Egypt. What do you value most? If you don't decide, other people will make that decision for you. The world's value system is what it has always been:

- Pleasure: I want to feel good.
- Possessions: I want to be wealthy.
- Power: I want to be popular and influential.

By the world's standards Moses had it made. Moses had

everything people wanted. He walked away from it all to live among slaves. Who would do that? Someone with a different value system! He realized there was something more valuable. He decided that God's purpose is more valuable than popularity. Listen, kings come and go, earthly kingdoms rise and fall, but he who does the will of God has eternal blessing.

He decided that people were more valuable than pleasures and God's peace was more valuable than earthly possessions. You cannot buy happiness. Moses wanted something to live for; not simply more to live on.

Moses' faith in God enabled him to keep focused on the real goal. ***"...for he was looking to the reward. By faith he left Egypt, not fearing the wrath of the king; for he endured as seeing him who is unseen." (Hebrews 11:27)***

Moses focused upon God. He gave up prestige, pleasure and plenty, but he did not give up on his dream. His heart was set on eternal rewards that would not pass way. Faith knows that losing something worldly is not really loss. When you lay up treasures in heaven it's retained forever. Moses' name was removed from the balance sheet of Egypt but was written on an eternal, unlimited bank account in heaven and that was by far better. Egypt is now a third world country, but heaven is still in its rightful place.

There were five key words that described Moses' life: he refused, he chose, he regarded, he saw, and he endured. ***"Therefore, since we have so great a cloud of witnesses surrounding us, let us also lay aside every encumbrance and the sin which so easily entangles us, and let us run with endurance the race that is set before us, fixing our eyes on Jesus, the author and perfecter of faith, who for the joy set before Him endured the cross, despising the shame, and has sat down at the right hand of the throne of God." (Hebrews 12:1-2)***

• ***"Let us lay aside that which hinders (entangles)."*** That's refusing.

• ***"Let us run with endurance."*** That's endurance.

• ***"The race set before us."*** That's the purpose.

• ***"Fixing our eyes on Jesus."*** That's the vision.

Jesus is our great example. He looked beyond the pain of the cross to the profit of the cross. He went to the cross, not because it was easy, but because of what it would accomplish, because people are more important than pleasure. Jesus was fully committed to the Father's plan.

In America, thankfully, we know little about true hunger or that thirst for food or water. When we say we are hungry, we are saying it's noon and we haven't had anything to eat since breakfast. We can relate to the fact that hunger has to do with desire.

The Psalmist said, ***"Taste and see that the Lord is good."*** Once you taste God you will want more of Him. David was a man after God's own heart who walked in close communion with the Lord. He wrote in Psalm 23 that he knew God, God's protection, and His care. He had a zeal for God's house; He knew God intimately. Yet in Psalm 42:1-2 he cried out, ***"As a deer pants for the water brooks, so my soul pants for You, O God. My soul thirsts for God, for the living God."*** He was saying that the hunger and thirst never diminishes.

The Apostle Paul had three great visions of God. He saw what only four other men in the Bible saw. He got to see inside heaven prior to his death.Yet he said his greatest desire was, ***"That I may know Him and the power of His resurrection and the fellowship of His suffering." (Philippians 3:10)***

When the Prodigal Son was hungry, he went to feed on the husk of the food fed to pigs. But when he was starving he went to his father's home. Our culture is hungry so it snacks on any and everything. Our culture is said to be more open to spiritual things than at any time in our history. They are hungry and interested, but not starving.

I like Luby's Cafeteria. When I go down the line I often pass on some items because I don't want to limit my options. There may be something better in the line ahead. I find it possible to get to the end and have an empty plate because I did not commit. Why do I do that? Because I am hungry but not starving. If I were starving I would run to the meat and potatoes. Listen, most people are not starving so they are sampling things that make no sense. They fill us temporarily, but will never satisfy. It's like eating popcorn at the movie; it will fill you up but not for long; it does not satisfy.

Today millions of people "practice" a religion. But religion is like going to an amusement park. It might amuse and entertain but it gets you nowhere. You get off the roller coaster where you got on. People who only go to church are like someone with a painful disease who just wants to be relieved of the pain and doesn't want to bother with the cause. Church goers want some kind of ecstasy experience or spiritual feeling. That's the focus of the emerging church. It's like the philosophy of Wal-Mart giving them what they want at a price they can afford. The crowd wants the "ah" moment. The modern, contemporary church tries to help people find happiness, but seldom addresses the real issue. They seek only to dull the pain with an emotional high.

Righteousness means to be right with God. But our songs have moved away from, *"It is Well With My Soul,"* to *"I Could Sing Of Your Love Forever."* We should want to sing about God's love, but we can't really know it until it is well with our soul!! The only real happiness in life is to be right with God.

This points to two things: salvation and sanctification. Listen, you have to be saved, not just seeking to know about

God. The book of Hebrews addresses those who only seek but never come to salvation. The heart of unbelief will keep you in your sin. When one sees their sin and rebellion the Spirit of God draws them to Jesus, but the person must step across the line and acknowledge it is Jesus plus nothing else that can quench their thirst and satisfy their hunger. Jesus is not the number one god of your top ten; He is the only God.

Once I step across the line I want more and more of what God offers, not in religion, but in a relationship. Like Paul says in Philippians 1:9, ***"Our love abounds more and more."*** We seek the totality of God's righteousness. We desire to be conformed to the image of Christ. David said in Psalm 17:15, ***"I shall be satisfied, when I awake, in thy likeness."*** You could add, "And I will not be satisfied until I do."

You may say that doesn't make sense. It's a paradox. You're satisfied but never satisfied. Let me explain it like this. I like pie. I eat until I am full. I stop eating but I want more because what I have just eaten gave me a desire for more.

When I seek God's righteousness, He gives it. ***"He has satisfied the thirsty soul, and the hungry soul He has filled with what is good." (Psalm 107:9)*** Again he says, ***"But they who seek the Lord shall not be in want of any good thing. (Psalm 34:10)*** Then David adds in Psalm 23, ***"I shall not want…my cup overflows."*** Jeremiah said, ***"My people shall be satisfied with my goodness, declares the Lord." (Jeremiah 31:14)*** Jesus told the woman at the well, ***"Whoever drinks of the water that I will give him shall never thirst." (John 4:14)*** And then in John 6:35 Jesus says, ***"I am the bread of life; he who comes to Me will not hunger."***

Jesus satisfies and yet there is in the true disciple a blessed dissatisfaction that wants even more and will be satisfied only when we see Jesus Christ in heaven. The disciple has a consuming ambition, not for power, pleasure and possessions, but for righteousness.

How do you feed your hungry soul? You love the Word of God. Jeremiah said in Jeremiah 15:16, ***"Your words were found and I ate them."*** The true disciple of Jesus has an unconditional hunger. Remember the rich young ruler who told Jesus that he wanted to know from Jesus how to get into the kingdom of God, but was unwilling to give up his possessions? His hunger was conditional, and he was never filled. He was just sampling religious appetizers. You can't have Christ and your sin, Christ and your pride, Christ and your illicit relationship, Christ and your cheating and lying, or Christ and your covetousness or materialism. A hungry man does not want food and a new set of clothes; he just wants food and water. David said, ***"My soul is crushed with hunger after your ordinances at all times." (Psalm 119:20)*** Isaiah also said in Isaiah 26:9, ***"At night my soul longs for you, indeed, my spirit within seeks You diligently."***

God always meets a man at the point of his desires. He will do just as much for a man as the man desires Him to do. He is as close to God as he wants to be. The beautiful thing about God is this, "You can have all of God you want." You may not be able to get all the money you want, or have your fill of material things, but you can have all of God you want; no matter what your circumstance or condition. That's why David said if we delight ourselves in the Lord He will give us the desires of our heart. No matter what is going on in our lives, God meets us at the point of our desires, but He will not go any further than what we desire. He works in our life according to the desires of the heart.

In the third chapter of the book of Revelation, Jesus wrote to the church at Laodocia that He loathed them because they had lost their desire for God. They felt they could be satisfied with wealth, but they could not. Jesus said in Revelation 3:16-17, ***"So because you are lukewarm, and neither hot nor cold,***

I will spit you out of My mouth. Because you say, 'I am rich, and have become wealthy, and have need of nothing,' and you do not know that you are wretched and miserable and poor and blind and naked..."

When a person says I have need of nothing, it means he is not hungry for God. That's our world in the United States. Why are we not hungry for God? We don't feel like we need God. We are like the rich man who prospered and had to build more storage buildings to hold all his stuff. Jesus said he was a fool because with all his stuff he did not have what he needed most; a relationship with God. That attitude makes God sick.

Because God loves us, He works in our lives to help create an appetite for Him. He usually does this through circumstances. ***"You shall remember all the ways which the Lord your God has led you in the wilderness these forty years, that He might humble you, testing you, to know what was in your heart, whether you would keep His commandments or not. He humbled you and let you be hungry, and fed you with manna which you did not know, nor did your fathers know, that He might make you understand that man does not live by bread alone, but man lives by everything that proceeds out of the mouth of the Lord." (Deuteronomy 8:2-3)***

God did what he did in the wilderness, letting the people fail for 40 years so that they might become hungry for Him. God was bringing them to a point of desperation so they would cry out to the Lord, "God, I am hungry for you."

If a man is a disciple he will have a spiritual appetite for God. If you don't desire God, if you don't want God, you are not a disciple. You may be religious, but you are not a true disciple of Jesus. The people who have no hunger for God and for His will are people who have never really tasted God. ***"...like newborn babies, long for the pure milk of the word, so that by it you may grow in respect to salvation, if you have***

tasted the kindness of the Lord." (1 Peter 2:2-3) If you have tasted the grace of the Lord you will be like a baby wanting milk. So if you do not desire God you may be a creation of God, but not a child of God.

Jesus said blessed are those who hunger and thirst to be right with God. Being righteous is to be right with God. The disciple is not hungry for a bite of God. They want all of God. The religious person wants a bite. They will attend an hour, maybe two hours a week out of religious duty. They want a slice of being right with God. They are lukewarm. They seek to be right in one area and disregard the rest. They go to church and they think because of this that they have paid their due and God will overlook their violent anger or an immoral encounter the rest of the week. That's being lukewarm. They may tithe to justify cheating on their taxes. There is an absence of love for God and compassion for what He loves. No one would bring a prayer request to them because they are not real. They are immature. They are like children who, when left to themselves, only eat candy and drink soda. They are self-centered, cranky, complainers, never grateful for what they have, always wanting their own way. What's wrong? They have an appetite, but are eating the wrong things. Only Jesus can truly make a person happy.

So how do you know you are hungry for God? What will be right in your life? First, you will be characterized by having the right affections. ***"Do not store up for yourselves treasures on earth, where moth and rust destroy, and where thieves break in and steal. But store up for yourselves treasures in heaven, where neither moth nor rust destroys, and where thieves do not break in or steal; for where your treasure is, there your heart will be also."(Matthew 6:19-21)*** You will love what God loves. You will live with an eternal perspective. The treasures of this world are vulnerable to the smallest things. They are only temporary. If you bank on this world you will suffer foreclosure. There is no security in this world. You are a fool to trust in a passing, dying world.

Secondly, this person will be right in their allegiance. ***"No one can serve two masters; for either he will hate the one and love the other, or he will be devoted to one and despise the other. You cannot serve God and wealth." (Matthew 6:24)*** No man can serve God and material things. Everyone lives by faith in something; that is how we operate. We all trust in something and are slaves to something. Jesus said we will either trust God or the physical realities of this life. That's why so many are so frustrated. My grandmother used to say they only have enough of God to bug them but not bless them.

The word despise means to underestimate or under value. You will hold tight to one and let your grip go to the other. Natural man always gravitates to the lesser, never the greater. Our world under values God so they don't trust in God. They think the world offers more than God. Religious people are Christians on Sunday and pagans on Monday. We sing about how we trust and love God, then on Monday act as if God does not exist.

Finally, the true disciple is right in his ambitions. ***"But seek first His kingdom and His righteousness, and all these things will be added to you." (Matthew 6:33)*** Our one ambition is the desire to please God in every area of our life; to want God's rule in our life. It places Jesus as the number one priority for our life. Then and only then will we be satisfied. Now when you are filled there is no room for anything else. Paul said, ***"I have learned that no matter what my outward conditions, I am content."(Philippians 4:11)*** Why? Because Jesus was the priority of his life. Paul wanted the Kingdom of God more than anything. The Kingdom of God is not just heaven; it is the sphere of God's rule. A true disciple such as

Paul was given over to be a kingdom builder.

The marks of a disciple of Jesus are a pursuit of righteousness, and the mentality of sacrificing for God and God's kingdom. That does not mean a desire to blow up buildings and die a martyr. It is far easier to die for a religious idea than to live a life of righteousness. The true disciple is not about hurting people in the name of religion or obeying a list of legalistic rules. It is to love what God loves.

The disciple of Christ is hungry for holiness, not happiness. Did you know that happiness is the by-product of seeking God? If you make happiness your goal in life, you are going to miss it because you can't find it by looking for it; it comes only as a result of knowing God. ***"Thus says the Lord: 'Let not the wise man glory in his wisdom, let not the mighty man glory in his might, nor let the rich man glory in his riches; but let him who glories glory in this, that he understands and knows Me, that I am the Lord, exercising lovingkindness, judgment, and righteousness in the earth. For in these I delight,' says the Lord. (Jeremiah 9:23-24)*** Contrast that to the reality of most people. ***"Why spend your money on what is not bread, and your labor on what does not satisfy?" (Isaiah 55:2)***

People are always looking for the quick fix. There is a plant in Australia called the, "Nordo" plant. Its spores are used to make bread and stew, but it has no minerals, no carbohydrates, no vitamins or protein that are essential for sustaining life. You can fill your stomach with it and die with a full stomach. What a picture of our culture.

I conduct many funerals. It is absolutely heartbreaking to hear what summed up the average person's life: They had a passion for sports; they loved to cook, and the list goes on with trivial pursuits of life that have no eternal impact. There is seldom a testimony for their love for Christ and their work for the kingdom. I am now referring to people who spent their lives attending church. God help us!

Jesus said, ***"I am the bread of life. Whoever comes to me will never go hungry and whoever believes in me will never be thirsty…if anyone eats of this bread he will live forever." (John 8:35; 51)*** That's what I call wonder bread! In biblical culture bread was the basic essential of life. It still is today. When there is a famine in a land, the first thing other countries do is to send flour to make bread. Jesus is saying, I am the most basic need a person has; I am foundational to real life; I am essential.

The emerging church mentality is to find happiness within yourself. Listen, when you are hungry, you don't tell your stomach to feed itself. That is so foolish; you have to have an outside source. It's time the church examines itself. David prayed, ***"Search me, O God, and know my heart. Test my thoughts, point out anything you find in me that makes you sad." (Psalm 139:23)***

Some might say I'm a Christian, but I am not hungry now. I have been in the past, but I have lost my appetite for God. Listen, a loss of appetite indicates illness. When a person is sick they usually are not hungry. The healthy disciple of Jesus is hungry for God!

~A Heart Of Compassion~

"Blessed are the merciful for they shall receive mercy." (Matthew 5:7)

The Beatitudes grow out of one another. It all began with being poor in spirit. When we have poverty of spirit and we realize that we are nothing but beggars, we will be willing to give to another beggar, so we will be merciful.

When we mourn over our sin, we wash our hearts pure with the tears of penitence, and we will be pure in heart.

When we are meek, we will be peacemakers, because meekness makes peace.

And when we are hungry and thirsty for righteousness, we will be willing to be persecuted for righteousness' sake. ***"But whoever has the world's goods, and sees his brother in need and closes his heart against him, how does the love of God abide in him? Little children, let us not love with word or with tongue, but in deed and truth." (1 John 3:17-18)***

Mercy is special. It is more than forgiveness. It is less than love. It is different from grace. And it is one with justice. The merciful are not only hearing the insults of evil men, but their heart also reaches out to them in compassion. The merciful one is sympathetic. They are forgiving. They are gracious and loving. They are not sentimental in that they allow sin to go unpunished or unconfronted just because someone is sad or upset.

David wrote in Psalm 37:21, ***"The wicked borroweth, and payeth not again, but the righteous showeth mercy."*** When one of my sons came to me and said, "I have done something wrong," and said they were sorry, then I was merciful, but if they lied about it I tended to show more punishment than mercy. Mercy gives acceptance, but not necessarily approval.

It was mercy in Joseph's life after being treated so badly by his brothers that caused him to accept them and meet their needs.

In Psalm 109:14-16 we read about the person without mercy, ***"Let the iniquity of his fathers be remembered before the Lord, and do not let the sin of his mother be blotted out. Let them be before the Lord continually, that He may cut off their memory from the earth."*** Why is this? Because he did not remember to show lovingkindness (that's mercy), but instead persecuted the afflicted and needy man, and the despondent in heart, to put them to death.

The merciful are those who reach out, not those who grasp and take. God help us to be able somehow to overrule a corrupt society and hear the voice of our God who tells us to give everything we have.

If someone offends us, we should be merciful. We should be compassionate, benevolent, sympathetic, and understanding. I learned a long time ago that understanding other people is the key to being merciful toward them. For example, if I am driving on the Interstate and a car cuts across four lanes of traffic to an exit ramp, barely missing my car and several others, my first inclination is to be angry and wish law enforcement would arrest them for reckless driving, but on the other hand if I knew their child was in the hospital emergency room at the point of death, I would certainly not be angry. As a matter of fact, I would want him to have a police escort.

If someone makes a mistake of a misjudgment or fails to pay a debt or return something they've borrowed, be merciful. We must live with the character of the kingdom.

Solomon wrote, ***"The merciful man does himself good, but the cruel man does himself harm." (Proverbs 11:17)*** Do you want to be really miserable? Be merciless! Do you want to be happy? Be merciful. Again, Solomon says, ***"The righteous man regardeth the life of his beast, but the tender mercies of the wicked are cruel." (Proverbs 12:10)*** He notes that righteous people are even merciful to animals. The wicked are cruel to everything.

Do you want to know the character of a godless culture? ***"...being filled with all unrighteousness, wickedness, greed, evil; full of envy, murder, strife, deceit, malice; they are gossips, slanderers, haters of God, insolent, arrogant, boastful, inventors of evil, disobedient to parents, without understanding, untrustworthy, unloving, unmerciful..." (Romans 1:29-31)*** Yet even to the godless world in which we were or are a part of, God gives mercy. God is the source of mercy. Mercy is not a human attitude. I'm not saying there is no kindness in our world, but even kindness is rude. Why? Because the only way to have mercy is to have the righteousness of God that comes through Christ. That's what Jesus is saying. If we come by this Beatitude path to the place of hungering and thirsting for righteousness, to be filled by God, we will know mercy.

People want the <u>blessing</u>, but they don't want the <u>belonging</u>. They are like Balaam, the false prophet who said, ***"Let me die the death of the upright." (Numbers 23:10)*** One commentator said it right, *"Balaam wanted to die like the righteous all right; he just didn't want to live like the righteous."* The only people who have mercy are the people who have come with a broken spirit before a holy God and have sought His righteousness.

The Psalmist said, ***"As the heaven is high about the earth, so great is his mercy toward them that fear Him." (Psalm 103:17)*** We fear God, we come to Christ and God gives us His mercy. Nothing can rival the cross for mercy, for it fulfilled Christ's role as a merciful High Priest. ***"Therefore, He had to be made like His brethren in all things, so that He might become a merciful and faithful high priest in things pertaining to God, to make propitiation for the sins of the people." (Hebrews 2:17)***

How does mercy act?

• The person of mercy is one who is always ready to forgive.

• The person of mercy will give themselves to meet the needs of others.

• The person of mercy is kind in their criticism and judgment of others.

"Do not judge so that you will not be judged. For in the way you judge, you will be judged; and by your standard of measure, it will be measured to you. Why do you look at the speck that is in your brother's eye, but do not notice the log that is in your own eye? Or how can you say to your brother, 'Let me take the speck out of your eye,' and behold, the log is in your own eye? You hypocrite, first take the log out of your own eye, and then you will see clearly to take the speck out of your brother's eye." (Matthew 7:1-5)

God commands us not to judge people. That does not mean we are not to call sin, sin. If I see a man robbing the convenience store, I am not judging him to be a thief, He is a thief. If a man smells of alcohol and his speech is slurred and he can't walk straight, I am not judging him to say he is drunk.

The word judge means "personal condemnation." It is discerning a person's motive. Listen, no one can look at another person's heart and rightly discern why they are doing or not doing something. I am not to condemn someone's motive. It speaks against perpetual fault finding.

When Jesus says don't do something He is really saying,

"Don't hurt yourself." A lack of mercy always brings its own consequences. So the true disciple is merciful. But why it is so important?

First of all, when I don't show mercy I expose myself to that same judgment. The moment I start exposing others in judgment God exposes me. ***"The good man brings out of his good treasure what is good; and the evil man brings out of his evil treasure what is evil. But I tell you that for every careless word that people speak, they shall give an accounting for it in the day of judgment. For by your words you will be justified, and by your words you will be condemned." (Matthew 12:35-37)*** The Bible warns us again and again to keep a watch over our mouth. In the book of Proverbs when God lists the seven things He hates, two of them have to do with the tongue. James speaks more about the misuse of his tongue than anything else. It makes me wonder about the gossips in the church, if they are even in a relationship with Christ. When I demand perfection from others, that same demand is placed on me by God.

Secondly, when I judge others I raise the standard of my own judgment. It means God demands a higher standard for us. When I deal with others without mercy, God deals with me in like manner. Mercy is not getting what I deserve. Aren't you glad God gives us mercy, not only at salvation, but everyday. I am! I don't know about you, but I want my mistake covered up with <u>love</u>. I am glad the Lord is my judge and not man. ***"In this case, moreover, it is required of stewards that one be found trustworthy. But to me it is a very small thing that I may be examined by you, or by any human court; in fact, I do not even examine myself. For I am conscious of nothing against myself, yet I am not by this acquitted; but the one who examines me is the Lord. Therefore do not go on passing judgment before the time, but wait until the Lord comes***

who will both bring to light the things hidden in the darkness and disclose the motives of men's hearts; and then each man's praise will come to him from God. (1 Corinthians 4:2-5) With greater status comes greater responsibility in the economy of God. ***"Let not many of you become teachers, my brethren, knowing that as such we will incur a stricter judgment." (James 3:1)*** To whom much is given, much is required. So when my judgment of others is harsher and without mercy, God's demand is greater holiness on my part.

Finally, we must be merciful, rather than judgmental because we are incapable of judging others. You know why? Because I judge you according to myself and I am not a good judge of perfection. Sin has obscured my ability to discern. I am like a blind eye doctor trying to perform eye examinations. Listen, only God knows the human heart. It is put in me for God's grace and I am not where someone else is. I have sin in my own heart. In John 8 a woman was brought to be stoned because of immorality. The law demanded death and Jesus said in effect let's fulfill that law, but let him who is without sin cast the first stones! There was one there that day who could rightfully have cast a stone, but He did not do it. His name is Jesus. That's mercy! Mercy is when you have caught them in their sin, you have the stone in your hand and the right to throw it, and you don't! That's mercy. God says I will bless you the way you are willing to bless others. Isn't it strange how God let's us determine our own blessings, and how we hold in our own hands the fate of our own judgments?

We are called to a life of mercy. We are to demonstrate mercy physically and spiritually. Physically we are to be merciful by giving the poor money, the hungry food, the naked clothing, etc. This means Christians are to have a social consciousness about them. I want to be a man people can look up to, knowing I will never look down upon them.

Spiritually we are to look after people's spiritual needs through pity, prodding, prayer, and preaching. St. Augustine said, *"If I weep for the body from which the soul is departed, should I not weep for the soul from which God has departed?"* We are to have pity for lost souls. ***"...with gentleness correcting those who are in opposition, if perhaps God may grant them repentance leading to the knowledge of the truth..." (2 Timothy 2:25)*** There has to be the confrontation about sin before there can ever be realization of sinfulness. ***"...save others, snatching them out of the fire; and on some have mercy with fear, hating even the garment polluted by the flesh."(Jude 23)***

I am showing mercy when I pray for people. To intercede for others in prayer is the way of the true disciple. Having prayed for them I present the good news.

Preaching God's Word is an act of showing mercy. To be a messenger of the life-changing message is the nature of giving mercy. Jesus said to the disciples, ***"When the Holy Spirit has come upon you, you will be my witnesses..."*** **(Acts 1:8)** **"With the kind You show Yourself kind, with the blameless You show Yourself blameless..." (2 Samuel 22:26)** ***"For judgment will be merciless to one who has shown no mercy; mercy triumphs over judgment." (James 2:13)***

The first four Beatitudes were entirely inner principles; they dealt entirely with inner attitudes of the heart. But the last four Beatitudes are outward manifestations of the first four. Jesus' sermon was to religious people that majored on the externals. His message cut them to the heart and said holiness is not found simply in what a person does, but rather who a person is.

In Jesus' day mercy was considered a sign of weakness. But Jesus said to be merciful is a key to the true disciple's character. God has laws that are eternally fixed. One of God's laws is this: a person reaps what they sow. Jesus said His disciples have mercy from God because they give mercy to others. It is not the idea that if you are merciful everyone will be merciful back to you. That is wishful thinking. Jesus was the most merciful person who ever lived and people nailed Him to a cross. This is not some human virtue that brings its own reward. It is, when you are merciful to others that God will be merciful to you.

The disciple displays the nature of Jesus. If I want to define a disciple's life, I don't look at creeds, dogma, and statements of faith; I look at Jesus. A disciple of Jesus does what Jesus did. The Beatitudes are important because they define for us who real disciples of Jesus are.

Jesus had mercy; sympathy in its purest form. ***"So then, since we have a great High Priest who has entered heaven, Jesus the Son of God, let us hold firmly to what we believe. This High Priest of ours understands our weaknesses, for he faced all of the same testings we do, yet he did not sin. So let us come boldly to the throne of our gracious God. There we will receive his mercy, and we will find grace to help us when we need it most." (Hebrews 4:14-16)*** As we close this chapter let's focus on Jesus' nature as a merciful Savior so we may gain insight as to how mercy is displayed with other people.

As a disciple I must learn to be patient with those who are peculiar. Into every life a few weirdos must fall. The Bible says, ***"Encourage the timid, help the weak, and be patient with everyone." (1 Thessalonians 5:14)***

If I am to be patient with people, a mandate with which I usually struggle, I have to be intentional. I must learn something about them, looking beneath their behavior to their need. This means I have to invest in people by giving time to them.

Secondly, as a disciple I will forgive those who have fallen. Have you noticed it is easier to point a finger than lend a helping hand? It is easier to criticize than to sympathize. As disciples of Christ we understand Jesus came to rub it out, not rub it in. Jesus said, ***"Be ye therefore merciful, as your Father also is merciful." (Luke 6:36)***

Another mark of a disciple who shows mercy is that they will help those who are hurting. ***"Wherever you possibly can, do good to those who need it." (Proverbs 3:27)*** A disciple gives practical assistance. I don't know how I would get through life without the help of other Christians. Hopefully, I can help others in the same way that I receive help. That is showing mercy. John instructs us in 1 John 3:17-18, ***"If someone who is supposed to be a Christian has enough mercy to live well, and sees a brother in need but won't help him, how can God's love be in him? Let's stop just saying we love people...let's show it by our actions."*** John Wesley made a profound impact on his world He wrote,

"Do all the good you can,
By all the means you can,
In all the ways you can,
At all the times you can,
To all the people you can,
As long as you ever can."

Contrast that to our carnal culture. Flip Wilson, a comedian once said, *"I am what you call a, 'Jehovah bystander!'"*

Jesus demonstrates the highest characteristic of mercy. As a disciple of Jesus we must also show mercy by doing good to our enemies. He calls us to show mercy to others. Jesus said, ***"If you do good to those who do good to you, what credit is that to you? Even sinners do that...but love your enemies, do good to them...then your record will be great. Be merciful, just as your Father is." (Luke 6:33; 35-36)*** The best way to eliminate an enemy is to turn him into a friend. But that's so hard! So how do we begin to do this?

• Pity: The soul absent from God.

• Prodding: Instruct and encourage men to get right with God.

• Pray for them.

Now if you are anything like me, this last call is so beyond your nature. I can't go there on my own. I have to let Jesus in me, take this step. I can tell you some things that help me take baby steps in answering the call to be merciful to my enemies:

• Remember how much mercy God has shown to you. We tend to judge others by their worse faults and we tend to judge ourselves by our best intentions.

• Remember you are going to need more of God's mercy in the future.

"The man who makes no allowances for others will find no more made for himself." (James 2:13)

• Remember mercy makes us happy. Ben Franklin was right when he said, *"When you are good to other people you are best to yourself."* Solomon said it even better, ***"Your own soul is nourished when you are kind. It is destroyed when you are cruel." (Proverbs 11:17)***

~The Call To Be Holy~

"Blessed are the pure in heart for they shall see God." (Matthew 5:8)

The Pharisee would pray like this, "God, I thank you that I am not like other people…even like this tax collector." (Reference Luke 18:11). His standard was lower than himself. The fallacy of that is that if everybody keeps basing his own evaluation on one person lower, the whole thing spirals down until the ultimate standard will be the most rotten person alive.

When God set the standard for acceptable behavior, He did not say you had to be better than a publican or an immoral man. He said if you want to see God, you have to be pure in heart." In Matthew 5:48 Jesus said, ***"Therefore you are to be perfect, as your heavenly Father is perfect."*** That's the standard of the absolute holy, righteous, and only God of the universe.

Who will enter the kingdom? Who will go to heaven? Who is fit to enter God's presence? Who will be saved? Who will ever have a vision of God? Who will enter into His bliss? Only those who are pure in heart.

Now I wish Jesus would have said, "Those pure in body." But he did not. He said blessed are those who are pure in heart. The religious Pharisees' behavior was impeccable. They worked at keeping the rules, but they paid no attention to love, truth and mercy. Jesus told them they were far from God. ***"Woe to you, scribes and Pharisees, hypocrites! For you are like whitewashed tombs which on the outside appear beauti-***

ful, but inside they are full of dead men's bones and all uncleanness." (Matthew 23:27) The Pharisees were pure in body. Outwardly they were above reproach. They lived so and strived so because they thought that keeping rules was what pleased God. The truth is you can be pure in body and not be pure in heart. But if you are pure in heart you will be pure in body.

The word pure means to be unmixed; not just being clean. The word pure means, "what you see is what you get." To be pure means you are what you appear to be; to have no mixed motives.

What does it mean to be pure in heart? In the Bible, the heart is always seen as the inside part of a person, the seat of his or her personality. It refers to the thinking process. The heart is not specifically the emotions. When the Bible speaks of the emotion it often refers to the "bowels of compassion;" the "feeling in the stomach." The Jew expressed his feeling in terms of what he felt in his stomach.

The mind and the heart were really together. ***"As he thinketh in his heart, so is he." (Proverbs 23:7)*** Sometimes the heart does refer to the will and the emotion as they spin off from the intellect. The wisest man who ever lived, Solomon said, ***"Watch over your heart with all diligence, for from it flows the springs of life." (Proverbs 4:23)*** Everything is generated from the heart.

God is after a changed heart. David cried out to God in Psalm 81:10, ***"Create in me a clean heart, O God."*** In Psalm 73:1 he says, ***"Surely God is good to Israel. Ah, but who is Israel? Those who are pure in heart."***

If you go to church every week, carry your Bible and even recite verses, but your heart is not clean, you have not met God's standard. For example, when God gave Israel a king they selected Saul because of his appearance. God gave Saul a good heart (1 Samuel 10:9). But Saul began to disobey God and it got to the place where Samuel came to him and said in effect, "Saul, the Lord says you are finished." Why? ***"The Lord has sought out for Himself a man after his own heart." (1 Samuel 13:14)***

Why does God care about that? The answer is in 1 Samuel 16:7, ***"For man looks at the outward appearance, but the Lord looks at the heart."*** Who was the man after God's own heart? David. God selected him because his heart was right. David said in Psalm 9:1, ***"I will give thanks to the Lord with all my heart." "Let the words of my mouth and the meditation of my heart be acceptable in Your sight, O Lord, my strength and my Redeemer." (Psalm 19:14) "Examine me, O Lord, and prove me; try my mind and my heart." (Psalm 26:2) "When You said, 'Seek My face,' My heart said to You, 'Your face, Lord, I will seek.'" (Psalm 27:8)***

Here was a man who was ruled from his heart. David sought God in his innermost being. And do you know what the sum of it all is? His heart was fixed upon God. ***"My heart is steadfast, O God, my heart is steadfast." (Psalm 57:7)*** David did fail on the outside, but not when his heart was set toward God.

A man's life is controlled by his heart. The preacher in Hebrews speaks of those who have a heart of unbelief. An unbelieving heart condemns a man, no matter what he looks like on the outside.

In the sermon Jesus says it is possible to do a good act in an evil way. In Matthew Chapter Six, Jesus looks at what men do religiously and says beware how you do them. He lists three acts of the religious. They are considered righteous acts.

- Acts of mercy.
- Acts of prayer.
- Acts of fasting.

These are religious acts, but not necessarily righteous acts from a pure heart.

To be pure in heart I must have a consciousness of the presence of God. Jesus says to keep from being impure in your religious life you have to understand God is your audience. The religious Pharisees were more aware of the presence of man than of God. Therefore, they did what they did publicly. They wanted the praise of man; they wanted to impress man. This type of person is unconscious of God's presence. Because of this they are hypocrites.

The pure in heart are becoming physically what they are spiritually. God hates pretense. In Acts 5 the couple who lost their lives, lost them because of pretense. God took their lives because they were pretending to be more than they were. They were passing off partial surrender as total surrender.

The hypocrites did religious things to be seen of men. Why? They wanted to impress men. That's why Jesus said we are to do our religious service in secret. Our focus is to be in pleasing God, not man. Why? We must be content with the praise of God above. Listen, no one can please everyone but we can please God.

Pleasing God is like making an investment. The reward may not be immediate but it will come. Most of us have a tendency to want immediate gratification. We sell out the future for the present. Why? Because what is a reward to a spiritual person is not seen as a reward by a carnal person. The reward for a spiritual person is simply that God is pleased with them. I want to be a pleasure to God!

How can your heart be made pure? Know you can't do it on your own; that's the first step. Acts 15:9 says that our hearts are cleansed by faith. You cannot do it by works, but you can by believing. In what? In the blood of Jesus Christ, which cleanses us from sin. The Apostle John says, ***"If we walk in***

the light as He Himself is in the light we have fellowship with one another, and the blood of Jesus His Son cleanses us from all sin." (1 John 1:7)

Do you want to be pure in heart? We must come to Christ in faith. There is no other way. If you do Jesus said you will "see God." We will live in the very presence of God. You will comprehend Him, you will realize that He is there, you will see Him with spiritual eyes. Like Moses who cried, ***"I pray you show me your glory." (Exodus 33:18)*** The one pure in heart sees that God is real. They don't just believe in God, they can believe God!

The problem in our culture is not that we are unconcerned about purity; it's we want everything pure but our hearts. In the United States we spent over a half billion dollars last year on water purifiers. This does not even take into account what we spent on bottled water. It seems we have missed the most important area of purification, the heart! Jesus said happiness is a heart condition. No wonder our culture is filled with so many people who confess they are void of any real happiness.

The ultimate goal of the majority of people is to see God and to be in heaven in the afterlife. A person does not even have to attend church to want that. Jesus agrees that wanting to see God should be our ultimate goal, and He tells us how we can live so that will be a reality.

The eye sees what it is trained to see. Have you looked at a computer-generated picture that is not a picture until you focus your eye upon it in a certain way? When they first came out I could not see the picture behind the computerized dots. It just looked like a bunch of dots on paper. Finally I saw it in another dimension. Beneath the dots were dinosaurs, birds, etc. Once I trained my eye to look with a certain focus, I could see them all. I could form the picture to another, seeing clearly the picture within the frame.

When we go to the doctor he many times looks at x-rays that were taken. All I can see is black and white, but in his trained eye he sees abnormalities and the source of illness and disease. What is true physically is also true spiritually. Two people can attend the same worship service; one can leave with a blessing and say, "I saw the Lord's hand at work today," and the other may have just thought the service would never end. One sits there and says, "Amen," the other, "So what."

Jesus said the mark of a true disciple; the secret of being happy is having the ability to see God; to be able to trace His hand at work in your life and in your world. When I can see God I know everything is going to be OK. The key to seeing God is having a pure heart, a heart of unmixed motives.

As already stated, Jesus is not talking about the organ in our body we call, "the heart." The word heart in this verse refers to the "thinking process." Apart from God our thinking process always takes men away from God. Listen to God's commentary on mankind after Adam's fall, ***"And God saw that the wickedness of man was great in the earth, and that every imagination of the thoughts of his heart was only evil continually." (Genesis 6:5)*** Jesus was speaking of man in his fallen nature when he said, ***"...for out of man's heart proceeds evil thoughts, murders, adulteries, fornications, thefts, false witness, blasphemies..." (Matthew 15:19)*** The Psalmist prayed, ***"Let the word of my mouth, and the meditation of my heart be acceptable in thy sight oh, God, my strength and my redeemer." (Psalm 19:14)***

So Jesus says, ***"As a man thinketh in his heart so is he." (Proverbs 23:7)*** Our lives are controlled by our hearts. To be pure in heart is to have unmixed devotion to God, an unmixed motivation to please God alone. It is to have spiritual integrity before God and a singleness of heart. This goes beyond motives alone. It is possible to have pure motives and not come to God. When the prophets of God challenged Elijah at Mount Carmel they cut them themselves with knives. They were very sincere. Terrorists who blow themselves up in the name of religion are very sincere. A pure heart, however, produces right motives and right actions; both have to be present. It is having our practical living match our divine position before God. It is being the same on the inside as you are on the outside. Only then are you real!

As a disciple of Jesus, we must continually develop a pure heart. The Sermon on the Mount tells us how to do that. It begins by understanding God sees everything. Three times Jesus says, ***"Your Father in heaven sees what you do in secret."***

In order to keep from being impure in your religious activities Jesus warns, we must be conscious of God's presence. Most people think that they can fool God. The Bible warns us, ***"Nothing in all creation is hidden from God's sight. Everything is uncovered and laid bare before the eyes of Him to whom we must give an account." (Hebrews 4:3)*** One may fake out others, but they cannot fake out God.

Secondly, we must continually review our motives. ***"God knows and judges your motives. He keeps watch over you. He knows and He will reward you according to what you do." (Proverbs 24:21)*** In Gods way of doing things our reward is not based on just <u>what</u> we do, but also on <u>why</u> we do it. Jesus tells us that the most basic religious activities of, giving, praying, and fasting, are done wrongly if we are not more aware of God's presence than people's presence. The point is when we are involved in religious activities, if we can't keep it a secret; we need to check our motives. It may be we want the praise of man more than the praise of God. Don't be a hypocrite. It is the opposite of the pure in heart. Who do you want to please the most? Paul said of himself, ***"We do not come to***

please others, but to please God who knows us through and through." (1 Thessalonians 2:4)

When you do religious things for man's praise, you will get it, but that is all you're going to get.

Thirdly, we must realign our priorities. Moses says of God, ***"You shall have no other god's before me." (Exodus 20:3)*** That is the first of the Ten Commandments. God says nothing is to be a god in your life. A god is anything that rivals our devotion and commitment to God. A god is anything we place before God in our life. It can be anything, good or bad.

How do we know if our hearts are pure? We must examine our activities. Where do we invest our time and money? Jesus said, ***"Don't pile up treasure on earth...but keep your treasure in heaven, for where your treasure is, <u>your heart</u> will be there too!" (Matthew 6:19)*** Where a person invests their time and money is where their heart is. It is easy to say, "God is first place in my life," but the truth is easily determined by looking at our checkbook and schedule.

Having examined our activities, then we need to look at our anxieties. Jesus said, ***"Therefore I tell you, don't worry about your life." (Matthew 6:25)*** Then Jesus deals with the five most common worries of life.

- Our finances. (Matthew 6:24)
- Our food. (Matthew 6:25)
- Our fitness. (Matthew 6:27)
- Our fashion. (Matthew 6:28)
- Our future. (Matthew 6:34)

When we worry it's because our focus has moved off of God on to lesser things. The disciple of Jesus is moving away from a consciousness of worldly circumstances, and on to a Christ-centered consciousness, trusting that God is in control, therefore, I don't have to be in control.

Finally, we must examine our ambitions, because our goals

reveal the direction of our hearts. Whatever is the number one goal in our lives is a god in our lives. Jesus said, ***"Don't worry about these things. This is what pagans are <u>always looking for</u> (ambitions). Your heavenly Father knows you need them. Instead <u>set your heart</u> first on His kingdom and His goodness and all these things will come to you as a matter of course." (Matthew 6:31-33)*** In the church it's hard to separate believers from the world because their activities, anxieties, and ambitions are the same as the pagan world. There is little difference because Christians have bought into the same value system. Jesus is saying the true disciple has set their heart on what God wants them to do and the other things in life will fall into place.

Allow me to sum up the heart of a true disciple. They are continually conscious of <u>God's presence</u> at all times. This is a mark of spiritual maturity. The more mature you are the more aware you are of God's presence and the less concerned you are of people and their opinions. True happiness comes down to one issue; who do you want to please?

The true disciple is content with <u>God's praise</u>. They want the reward of God, the smile of God upon their life, and the good hand of God upon them. A person gets only temporary reward from men, but eternal reward from God. Far too many in the church have sacrificed the eternal upon the altar of the immediate. Let's look at the contrast between Matthew 6:2 and 6:4. Verse two speaks of immediate reward, but verse four speaks of invested reward. Another mark of maturity is a willingness to wait for the greater reward.

Disciples are also controlled by <u>God's priorities</u>. In other words, they set their heart on what's of eternal importance. We must develop an eternal perspective. No wonder David prayed to God, ***"Create in me a new clean heart, oh God, fill me with clear thoughts and right desires." (Psalm 73:1)*** What best describes your heart?

- A broken heart with all its hurts.
- A cold, hard heart filled with bitterness.
- A divided heart that goes to church on Sunday and lives like the devil on Monday.
- A clean heart that sees God's work in your life daily.

Jesus says happiness is a heart condition. Are you truly happy in Jesus?

~Reconciling Our World~

"Blessed are the peacemakers for they shall be called the sons of God." (Matthew 5:9)

"Now all these things are from God, who reconciled us to Himself through Christ and gave us the ministry of reconciliation, namely, that God was in Christ reconciling the world to Himself, not counting their trespasses against them, and He has committed to us the word of reconciliation. Therefore, we are ambassadors for Christ, as though God were making an appeal through us; we beg you on behalf of Christ, be reconciled to God."
(2 Corinthians 5:18-20)

In the Beatitudes Jesus is not discerning eight different people, but rather one person who is truly a disciple of Jesus. The new birth brings a new nature. At spiritual birth we receive a new DNA. We are a new creation. Therefore, we live in a different way; we have a new walk, and a new value system. We have been changed! We are called to be salt and light. The question is does our presence make a difference in our world? As a disciple of Christ we should be like light in the darkness, and medicine to the sick. In this Beatitude Jesus does not say we are to be peace lovers, but peacemakers. We are to affect the world by bringing reconciliation in our world.

Making peace is not just about ending wars; it is about

bringing God's blessings to our world. Peace is not defined by the absence of conflict or strife. No conflict or strife exists in a cemetery, but we don't look for a model of God's peace there. As God sees it, peace is far more than the absence of something. It is the presence of righteousness that causes right relationships. Peace is not just stopping war; peace is creating righteousness that brings enemies together in love.

There is a big difference between a truce and peace. A truce just says we are reloading. Peace comes when the truth is known, the issue is settled, and the parties embrace each other. How different is this from our world's desire? In our world, we often exalt the people who break peace, not the ones who make it. Have you noticed that? We will pay a lot of money to watch two men in a ring beat each other to a pulp. Worldly kingdoms always give the highest honor to the warrior. We bow to the god of macho, the hard nosed, tough guy who takes nothing from anyone. These are the heroes of a fallen culture.

We are a culture who fights for our rights, exalting ourselves. It's no wonder that when Christians try to bring the peace of the gospel to their culture, they are fought.

Why should I seek to be a peacemaker as a disciple? First of all, it is indispensable to my own relationship to God. God is about relationships with Him and with others. Jesus says if you are out of fellowship with people in your life, you are out of fellowship with Him. ***"Therefore if you are presenting your offering at the altar, and there remember that your brother has something against you, leave your offering there before the altar and go; first be reconciled to your brother, and then come and present your offering." (Matthew 5:23-24)*** ***"…what we have seen and heard we proclaim to you also, so that you too may have fellowship with us; and indeed our fellowship is with the Father, and with His Son Jesus Christ." (1 John 1:3)***

It is impossible for two people to be close to Jesus and not be closer to one another. God says He cannot accept our worship if we are at war with each other. The quality of the gift is determined by the quality of the giver. God looks at the heart. The acceptability of our worship before God is based on the heart of the one worshiping. We try to compensate for broken fellowship so we try to do more religious things. God does not necessarily want you to double your tithes, but He does want you to make peace with your brother. The power of the Holy Spirit was able to flow through the church in Acts because they were in one accord. They had unity. There is no substitute for unity in our fellowship.

Jesus said we are to take the initiative. That does not mean they will receive it, but Peter said, ***"If possible, so far as it depends on you, be at peace with all men." (Romans 12:18)*** Sometimes people don't cooperate, but that doesn't change the fact that we have to make the effort. Forgiveness is a choice, not a feeling. I choose to let it go. I can't forget but I can forgive. To forgive is to humble yourself. But remember when I humble myself God exalts.

Notice Jesus said to make peace immediately. Why? It does not take long for the root of bitterness to grow deep. The longer you wait, the harder it will be. That's why Paul said not to let the sun set on your anger.

When I meet the Lord in eternity I want to have short accounts. God has called disciples to be bridge builders. ***"Pursue peace with all men, and the sanctification without which no one will see the Lord." (Hebrews 12:14)*** When I am filled with the Holy Spirit He produces in me the fruit of peace. Until I have the peace with God and the peace of God I can't be a peacemaker. When I see such unforgiving hearts in the church I wonder if they know peace with God and the peace of God. Paul said the disciple has his ***"...feet shod with***

the preparation of the gospel of peace." (Ephesians 6:15) Peace is good news! That's why evangelism is at the heart of the peacemaker. We can help someone who is at war with God make peace with God. You say, but I am not at war with God! Well, if you don't have a relationship with God through faith in Christ alone, God is at war with you, and this is a war you cannot win. Evangelism is peacemaking. Every believer is called to share the good news!

The Beatitudes are not a description of eight types of people, but eight characteristics of a true disciple of Jesus Christ. It's not the idea that a disciple says, "I may not be meek, but I do have mercy." No, the Beatitudes define the character of those who are really disciples of Christ and not simply superficial, "Christ followers." These are the characteristics of the nature of Jesus.

You can always tell when Jesus is around. His presence always made a decided difference. When there was fear, He brought hope and peace; where there was sadness, He brought joy; and where there was death and despair, Jesus brought life. Jesus tells His disciples, ***"As the Father has sent Me, even so send I you." (John 20:21)*** God wants us to be kingdom builders, salt and light, and to display His nature in this fallen world.

Jesus is the Prince of Peace, but He was not a pacifist. The teaching of scripture never teaches believers that we are to have peace at any cost. In Romans 12:18 Paul says, ***"If it is possible, as far as it depends on you, live at peace with everyone."*** The cause of all conflict, whether between couples, countries, or countrymen, is the same. It is because of selfishness and self-centeredness. God calls this sin. In James 4:1-2 we see the root of all conflict. ***"What is the source of the wars and the fights among you? Don't they come from the cravings that are at war within you? You desire and do not have.***

You murder and covet and cannot obtain. You fight and war. You do not have because you do not ask." Solomon, the wisest man who ever lived said, ***"The effect of pride is fighting." (Proverbs 13:10)***

As long as pride is in the heart of fallen men, war will exist. There are times, according to scripture, that until sin is dealt with it is impossible to have peace. The disciple is not called upon to be a doormat that surrenders to be walked upon or to raise a white flag of surrender to the evil of the culture. Solomon says there is a time for peace and a time for war. (Reference Ecclesiastes 3).

So when is it right for the people of God to say no to peace at any cost? It is right to fight when war is the lesser of two evils. There are many times in scripture when God commanded the people of God to fight. Many of God's heroes of faith fought for God's glory and His name.

When Jesus was in His early ministry He never suggested to a Roman soldier to leave his post or run from his duty. As a matter of fact Jesus told His disciples, ***"You are going to hear of wars and rumors of wars. See that you are not alarmed, because these things must take place, the end is not yet." (Matthew 24:6)***

There will always be wars until Jesus returns. Twice Jesus cleansed the temple by force. One time Jesus told His disciples to sell their coats and buy a sword. (Reference Luke 22:36). The Bible again and again tells us we are to resist certain things. We are not to sit passively back and accept evil. We are to resist it.

It is right to fight to preserve freedom. In Numbers 32 God is very upset with two tribes of Israel because they were unwilling to go to war with their countryman. Moses asked, ***"Are you just going to sit here?"*** As a disciple of Jesus we have to decide what's worth dying for. Until you know what's worth dying for you will never know what's worth living for. Some things are worse than war. God often commanded Israel to go liberate certain groups of people who were under evil dictators who held them under evil conditions.

God's people are called upon to defend innocent people. Solomon said, ***"When justice is done, it brings joy to the righteous, but terror to evil doers!" (Proverbs 21:5)*** Christians are not simply interested in peace. Certainly we work and pray for peace, but not at the expense of justice. Peace at any price is not peace; it's appeasement. I once heard someone say it well, *"All that has to happen for evil to triumph is for good men to do nothing."* A man that will only fight for his own personal cause is a miserable person.

It is right for a Christian to fight to stop the spread of evil. Paul said speaking of governments, "(The government) ***is there to serve God for your benefit. If you break the law, however, you may well have fear…he does not bear the sword for nothing. He is God's servant, an agent of justice to bring punishment on the wrongdoers." (Romans 13:41)*** The government was to be an agent of God to protect innocent people and bring justice to those who do evil, to enforce God's laws in our world. This includes capital punishment. The Ten Commandments do not literally say, "Thou shall not kill;" they say, "Thou shall not murder." There is a great difference in those two statements.

This world will know peace one day. It will not happen, however, until Christ returns. As you enter the United Nations there is a quote from Isaiah 2:4, ***"He will settle disputes among great nations. They will hammer their swords into plows and their spears into pruning knives. Nations will never again go to war, never prepare for battle again."*** It is the Messiah who will settle all conflict, not the United Nations.

You and I can do little to bring world peace, but we can do something. First of all, we can pray. The Bible says, ***"First of all pray…for kings and all others who are in authority, that we may live a quiet and peaceful life." (1 Timothy 2:1-2)*** We can pray for our political leaders, for our soldiers, and for our enemies.

Secondly, we must trust God. The Bible says, ***"The Lord is my light and my salvation, whom shall I fear? … though an army besiege me…and war break out against me, even then I will be confident." (Psalm 27:1; 3)***

Thirdly, we can seek peace. God commands us to seek peaceful solutions. ***"Turn from evil and do good. Seek peace and pursue it." (Psalm 34:14)*** This means we are to long for peace. We are to fight without hatred; resist without bitterness, and triumph without being proud.

Finally, we must support one another. We are to, ***"Carry each other's burdens…and fulfill the law of Christ." (Galatians 6:4)*** This means in our personal relationships we are to restore one another. What does this require of us on a personal level? It requires us to forgive those who have hurt us. The truth is, while it is natural to resent those who hurt us, resentment doesn't work. Job said, ***"To worry yourself to death with resentment would be a foolish, senseless thing to do." (Job 5:2)*** Resentment always hurts you more than the person being resented. Resentment makes people bitter and makes them sad. I have never met anyone who has said, "My bitterness has been such a blessing, it has been a real calming effect on my life." The truth is it makes one ugly on the inside and finds its way into every area of our life. The Bible says, ***"Never hold grudges; remember the Lord forgave you, so you must forgive others." (Colossians 3:13)***

Every child of God has experienced what we do not deserve; forgiveness from God! We have a tendency, however, to forget how much God has had to forgive us. We hate other people's sin, but overlook our own sin as not so bad.

Did you know the Bible teaches that on a personal level, unresolved conflict blocks our intimacy with God? It hinders our prayer life and our worship. ***"Husbands, likewise, dwell with them with understanding, giving honor to the wife, as to the weaker vessel, and as being heirs together of the grace of life, that your prayers may not be hindered." (1 Peter 3:7)*** ***"So if you are presenting a sacrifice at the altar in the Temple and you suddenly remember that someone has something against you, 24 leave your sacrifice there at the altar. Go and be reconciled to that person. Then come and offer your sacrifice to God." (Matthew 5:23-24)***

To become a peacemaker I must apply God's principles from His Word to my personal life. Notice the following biblical principles:

• Admit your hurt. You can't get over hurt until you are honest about it.

• Release the offender.

Peter asked Jesus, ***"How many times shall I forgive my brother when he sins against me, seven times?*** (The law required three). ***Jesus answered, not seven times, but seventy times seven." (Matthew 18:21-22)***

• Pursue God's peace.

Paul said, ***"And let the peace that comes from Christ rule in your hearts. For as members of one body you are called to live in peace." (Colossians 3:15)*** He further stated, ***"If you do this you will experience God's peace, which is far more wonderful than the human mind can understand." (Philippians 4:7)*** God transforms pain with peace. While I can't explain it, I can illustrate the principle. It's like not wanting to do something and when you do it you discover you really like it. That is what God does. Once you have experienced His peace you will want more of it. Paul prayed for the church, ***"May the Lord of peace Himself always give you His peace no matter what happens." (2 Thessalonians 3:16)***

God's peace has little to do with circumstances and a great deal to do with choice as to how we handle circumstances. God places His peace in our lives where no one or no thing can touch it, but Himself.

• Make amends if possible.

It's not always possible, but if we can, we are to do it with humility, without personal excuses and in a spirit of love.

I love what Job says in Job 11:13-16, ***"Put your heart right, reach out to God, then face the world again, firm and courageous, then all your troubles will fade from your ministry, like floods that are past and remembered no more."*** A peacemaker is one who is right with God. You can't be at peace with others if you don't have the peace with God, and the peace of God. A peacemaker reaches out to God. They know they can't do it without supernatural help. A peacemaker faces the world again with faith and courage. They know they will not resolve every disagreement, but they can reconcile their relationships with God's grace.

~Standing For Jesus~

"Blessed are those who are persecuted for righteousness' sake, for theirs is the kingdom of God." (Matthew 5:10)

Contrary to the carnal gospel preached in many churches today, being a true disciple of Jesus brings with it a cost. If we answer the call of God to be born into a personal relationship we will be blessed. We will be part of God's family, but such blessings will be followed also by persecution. But, if I faithfully go through that suffering, I will have the greater blessing. ***"Consider it all joy, my brethren, when you encounter various trials, knowing that the testing of your faith produces endurance. And let endurance have its perfect result, so that you may be perfect and complete, lacking in nothing." (James 1:2-4) "After you have suffered for a little while, the God of all grace, who called you to His eternal glory in Christ, will Himself perfect, confirm, strengthen and establish you." (1 Peter 5:10)***

All the virtues of the Beatitudes' character are intolerable to an evil world. The world cannot handle someone who is poor in spirit, because the world lives in pride, in a state of self-promotion, and ego substantiation. The world cannot tolerate mourning over sinfulness. It wants to bypass sin altogether and convince itself that it's alright. The world cannot tolerate meekness; it honors pride. The world cannot tolerate someone who knows he is nothing and seeks something that cannot be earned. The world knows little about mercy, purity, and making peace. These characteristics flagrantly counter the system.

When the world runs into real Christianity, there is always conflict, conviction, guilt, resentment, and persecution. If a disciple functions according to the first seven principles in the Beatitudes they inevitably will be persecuted for righteousness sake.

Notice first of all the reality of persecution. Jesus said you will be reviled. He did not say there is a possibility you will suffer, because you will suffer. Have you noticed how honest Jesus always is? When he called Paul in Acts 9, He said you are my chosen vessel, and by the way you will suffer many things because of it. Paul says in 1 Timothy 3:12, ***"Indeed, all who desire to live godly in Christ will be persecuted."*** That is a guarantee. Everyone who lives the Christ life will suffer. That's how it has always been and always will be.

You say I guess God just loves us more here in the United States because we know little of physical persecution. I read in scripture, however, that the disciples praised God that they were worthy to suffer for Jesus' sake. If we don't undergo persecution in our life, we had better examine our claim to being Christians. It may be that we are not counted worthy by God. Let me tell you one reason Christians are not being persecuted in the United States. It is because we have lowered the standard of righteousness. We have people who claim to be Christians who do not live enough of a righteous life to meet any honest definition of Christianity.

We think the world is more tolerant, but the fact is we may be living intolerable lives. We want to be popular; we want to be famous; we want to be acceptable. Listen, if we live the Christ life the world will oppose it.

Jesus said there are three kinds of persecution that real disciples will suffer. First, He said they will revile you. That means to be dishonored or discredited for being Christians. We see this all the time. Christians are disgraced in this culture. The world is made to believe the worst about God's people. The media always makes the Christian a radical fraud, or out of touch with the real world. If someone started a rumor about a Christian leader, most people would not even try to find out the facts. They would automatically believe it, even in the church. The world loves the gossip wire. It loves to believe the worst.

The word persecute means to follow, to put to flight. Christians live in glass houses. Remember when Jesus and the disciples were walking in the country and went through a cornfield? A couple of disciples ate some corn. All of a sudden the Pharisees accused them of breaking the Sabbath law! Let me ask you a question; what were they doing in a cornfield on the Sabbath? The answer to that is, they were following Jesus. They were persecuting him by watching him, happy to discredit him. That made them feel better about themselves.

Then Jesus said the world will lie about you. What's not true, the world will make up. Why? The world does not persecute Christians because they are good. They do it because they are different. The world accepts Christian goodness. They love our humanitarian efforts. You know why we are not persecuted much here in our country? It's because we're not much different than the culture. We might not be caught up in immorality but that is about the only difference in the modern church and our culture. If you start to live differently you will be persecuted, and it may start with people you know who attend church with you. It's often churchgoers who are the first to oppose the radical disciple's life. I know a young lady who has committed not to kiss a boy until she is married. It is church people who put her down and think she has lost her mind. Why? Because that idea is counter-cultural, even to people in the church.

What is the promise if we live differently from the world for the cause of Christ and suffer as a result? There is a cost but it's worth it. ***"For I consider that the sufferings of this present time are not worthy to be compared with the glory that is to be revealed to us." (Romans 8:18)*** Any loss here in this world can never be compared with the gain in God's kingdom. Twice Christ used the word blessed. Those who are willing to stand up for Jesus Christ will know the greater blessing of God's eternal kingdom.

Remember Stephen in the book of Acts? His last vision was looking into heaven and Jesus was standing. This is the only time in scripture where Jesus is standing in heaven. Here and every other place He is seated in a place of authority. It's worth repeating. Someone said, "When I stand for Jesus He will stand for me." What a truth!

If we are willing to pay the price now, God says the glory that shall be revealed is incomparable. Double blessed are the persecuted, for theirs is the kingdom and all that the kingdom could possibly contain. I think Christ is talking about here and now when the living King dwells within us and reveals and gives us the fullness of kingdom life spiritually.

In Mark 10:28 Peter said, ***"Behold, we have left everything and followed you."*** He was saying, "We've just done it Lord. We've stripped ourselves naked. We have given all to follow you." Christ answered Peter and the disciples in verses 29-30, ***"There is no one who has left house or brothers or sisters or mother of father or children or farms, for my sake and the gospel's sake, but that he will receive a hundred times as much now in the present age and in the age to come, eternal life."*** Blessed now and great blessing then; blessed here and now and then and there. It's all ours. What a fulfillment! We are so shortsighted. We want to protect the moment rather than give the moment to God and secure an eternal weight of glory.

While we are living in this fallen world, the disciple of Christ is fighting a spiritual war. Paul says, ***"We are not fighting against human beings, but against wicked spiritual forces…" (Ephesians 6:12)*** The disciples of Jesus are hated by Satan because they love the Lord Jesus. Satan can't get to God so He attacks what God loves, His children.

In the last chapter we discussed the fact that the disciple of Jesus is a peacemaker. This is very difficult to do when we are under attack. Our flesh wants to retaliate. Paul admonishes the Christian, ***"If someone does evil to you, don't pay him back with evil…never take revenge…let God's wrath do it." (Romans 12:17 & 19)*** We can trust God to settle the score. This present world is not all there is to our life. Paul went on to say, ***"Don't be overcome by evil, but overcome evil with good." (Romans 12:21)*** As a believer we never get ahead by getting evil. We must allow the Holy Spirit to control us and the Christ-life to prevail.

I'm not saying that we invite unnecessary pain into our lives. When the disciples were being attacked by their persecutors, they often fled. There is nothing cowardly about living to fight another day. When Peter was released out of prison by the angel following James' death, he went to where the disciples were praying for him. Then he left to avoid further persecution. When the persecutors wanted Paul dead after his conversion, he was lowered in a basket over the outside wall to escape them. Paul even used legal means to keep from being killed by a mindless coward.

Disciples are not looking for opportunities to be physically or emotionally persecuted, they are just living godly lives and that often brings persecution. When it comes they are able to rejoice in the midst of it. They don't rejoice for the pain, but because of their faith they know God's spirit rests upon them.

They rejoice because the world has seen Jesus in their life. Peter said, ***"Be happy if you are insulted for being a Christian for then the glorious spirit of God will come upon you." (1 Peter 4:14)*** The disciple also celebrates the persecution because they know it's only temporary. ***"These troubles...won't last very long. Yet this short time of distress will result in God's richest blessing upon us forever and ever." (2 Corinthians 4:17)*** Paul is saying the disciple's focus is not upon what is seen, but what is unseen.

When we live with an eternal perspective, name brands don't matter, things don't last in this world, it is passing away. This includes persecution. What is going to last is how we use our lives. God is taking account of our faithfulness. Paul reminds us, ***"Since we are God's children...if we share Christ's suffering, we will also share in His glory." (Romans 8:17)*** What a verse! WE are going to share in Jesus' glory. The Bible says, ***"For our light affliction, which is but for a moment, is working for us as far more exceeding and eternal weight of glory, while we do not look at the things which are seen, but on the things which are not seen. For the things which are seen are temporary, but the things which are not seen are eternal." (2 Corinthians 4:17-18)***

Going against our culture is taking the narrow road. I used to think the broad road and the narrow road Jesus talked about were two separate highways; one leading away from God to destruction, and the other leading to God to heaven. I now see them as one road. The broad road leading away from God, traveled by the majority and in the center of that road the narrow road going the opposite direction to heaven, but against the flow. By the very nature of going against culture it is a holy sand paper removing what is less like God so we can be more like Jesus. Solomon said, ***"Sometimes it takes a painful situation to make us change our ways." (Proverbs 20:30)***

Paul said, ***"I am glad…not because it hurts you, but because the pain turned you to God." (2 Corinthians 7:9)***

In the midst of persecution, God uses the pain to correct us, to direct us, to perfect us, and to protect us from something worse. Persecution in our lives helps us to learn many things. Let's look at some of these:

- It helps us learn to depend upon the Lord.

"We are crushed and overwhelmed…and saw how powerless we were to help ourselves, but that was good; for then we put everything into the hands of God, who alone could save us…and He did help us!" (2 Corinthians 1:8-10)

- We learn to obey God's Word.

When David was lamenting over his persecution he said, ***"It was the best thing that could have happened to me, for it taught me to pay attention to your law." (Psalm 119:71)***

- We learn we need other believers.

Again Solomon said, ***"Two people are better than one…if one falls down, the other can help him up. But it is bad for the person who is alone and falls, because no one is there to help." (Ecclesiastes 4:9-10)*** This truth is never so real as when we are being persecuted for righteousness sake. To have others' encouragement and support gives us the catalyst to keep moving forward rather than retreating.

The careful student of God's Word will recognize the pattern of the children of God when they faithfully proclaim the gospel and live the Christ life. There will be blessings, people will be transformed by the gospel, the world will persecute them, and then God will give the greater blessing. Stephen's sermon in Acts, Chapter 8 demonstrates that in the lives of Moses, Joseph, and Abraham. He told the non-believing world what they were doing to him is what the world has always done to the true people of God. Sadly most Christians don't want to endure the persecution so they miss God's greater blessing.

Stephen's circumstances in the Book of Acts reminds us of two things:

• God stands for persecuted people who are opposed because of their faith. When the world touches a child of God it's as if they are touching God.

When Jesus confronted Paul on the Road to Damascus He said, ***"Saul, why are you persecuting me?" (Acts 9:4)*** The converse is also true. In Matthew 25 Jesus taught that when Christians minister to the needy in His name by feeding them, giving them water and providing them housing or shelter, that it is as if they have ministered to Him. Jesus said, ***"Inasmuch as you did it to one of the least of these my brothers, you did it unto me." (Matthew 25:40)***

• Secondly, when you resist God's kingdom you will always lose. The Bible says God will not be mocked; the world reaps what it sows. Saul was there as Stephen was stoned; he was part of the crowd, guilty of Stephen's death. In the next chapter Paul's life was transformed. God can break the hardest rocks.

As I close this chapter, I feel I must address the truth that not all our pain comes from being persecuted because of righteousness. Make sure you are suffering for Jesus, and for the sake of the gospel, not because you are a jerk. There are things we call persecution that are not really persecution.

• Personality conflict is not persecution. It may mean that the pain in your life is simply because you are not popular. If you are loud, self-centered, egoistical, proud, and a controlling person, people don't want to be around you. I meet people who are loved by many, but no one likes to be around them.

• Integrity conflict in a person's life will bring its own set of issues. If you break the rules, the laws, and ethical standards, you are not being persecuted; you're being punished.

• If you are always focused on your rights and ignore public policy and find you are fired because of it, don't call that persecution; you are simply being reprimanded. For example, if you are a teacher in the public school system there are policies that all teachers have to abide by. A teacher can be salt and light; they can speak of their personal relationship with Christ, especially when asked, but they cannot preach a sermon to their students in class or have a come forward invitation. To be removed from the classroom is not persecution, it's policy. No one can do that in the class room.

Jesus said persecution will come into the life of a true disciple. We are not to be surprised by it; we are not to be discouraged by it, but we are to remember that when we stand for Jesus He stands for us.

Order more copies of

The Call to

Radical Discipleship

Are You Really A Christian?

Call toll free: 1-877-212-0933

Visit: www.crosshousepublishing.com

Email: crosshousepublishing@earthlink.net

FAX: 1-888-252-3022

Mail copy of form below to:

CrossHouse Publishing
P.O. Box 461592
Garland, Texas 75046

Number of copies desired ____________

Multiply number of copies by $ 9.95

Sub-total __________________

Please add $3 for postage and handling for first book and add 50-cents for each additional book in the order.

Shipping and handling$_____________

Texas residents add 8.25% sales tax $_____________

Total order $___________

Mark method of payment:

check enclosed _____________________________________

Credit card# _______________________________________

exp. date____ (Visa, MasterCard, Discover, American Express accepted)

Name ____

Address ____

City State, Zip ______________________________________

Phone _____________________ FAX ____________________

Email ____

Printed in the United States
205576BV00004B/280-471/P

9 781934 749210